Contents

Introduction

Know, therefore, that from the greater silence I shall return; Forget not that I shall come back to you; A little while, a moment of rest upon the wind, and another woman shall bear me.

Kahlil Gibran

Have you ever wondered who you were in a past life? You are not alone. Many of us have the feeling that we have lived other lifetimes. Reincarnation, which in Latin means "in flesh again," is the idea that the spirit is reborn into other physical bodies.

In most of the world's spiritual traditions, death is not seen as the end, but as part of an ongoing cycle. People in most all cultures agree that we are born, live, die, and then are reborn into another body. We cycle through our lifetimes just as nature cycles through the seasons. We have a spirit that transcends our physical body, and this spirit evolves over many lifetimes.

In the past few years, there has been an increased

interest in, and acceptance of, reincarnation. The first thing I did after deciding to write this book was begin reading through the vast amount of information on the subject. Besides being surprised by the volume of information, I was amazed at the number of cases of people having other lifetime experiences in different bodies. Many of the accounts were of children who at a very early age could remember another lifetime.

Even more amazing was that scientists and psychologists alike were actively investigating the idea of reincarnation. In doing so, they had gone to great lengths to verify these accounts by going to places and contacting people who were part of the reported previous lifetime. Reading the accounts of some of these children (for example, leading researchers to the right house of a past lifetime, and then correctly identifying most of the people associated with the previous life) confirmed that there was definitely something to the whole concept of reincarnation.

Everyday people have been known to have unusual experiences related to reincarnation and past or future lifetimes that are scientifically checked out, and seem to be real, at least on some level. As if people having these verifiable reincarnation experiences weren't enough to push the envelope, many of these other lifetime experiences also had a positive, healing effect on people's present lifetimes, both physically and psychologically. These healing effects went all the way from clearing away phobias to helping one person go from a nonfunctional mental patient to a functioning human being.

The idea that the soul is eternal and lives on forever is a part of most spiritual traditions, but the idea that people, when they die, reincarnate into other personalities is an essential part of reincarnation. The basic spiritual concept is that we all live through different lifetimes. Through action we evolve and work toward a balance between the polarities of birth, life, death, and rebirth. The idea in life is to move spiritually forward, revering our past as we constantly move beyond it. This is the basic foundation of reincarnation.

Each new generation brings another texture to the human landscape. Parading in new disguises we attempt to create and resolve energetic imbalances over the context of lifetimes. These are the influences that affect each of our lives—both in this lifetime and in terms of many lifetimes.

This book explores several cases of reincarnation as well as the philosophical and spiritual concepts that give reincarnation meaning within the whole of existence. Each lifetime affects every other lifetime. This is the foundation for the concept of karma. Rather than being about payback, karma is about cause and effect, and their relationship to each other, which overall is a state of balance.

The format of this book is straightforward and easy to absorb. Chapter One covers the basics of reincarnation while giving an interesting assortment of cases to support the ideas. Past lives is the focus of Chapter Two, surveying the ideas and work of many of the top researchers in the field. Chapter Three presents the ideas behind karma, both from Western and Eastern points of view, and how these ideas affect your present lifetime. Chapter Four moves everything into the future by exploring people who were visionaries, and relates these ideas to future life progression. Chapter Five concludes the book by providing ideas on how to integrate the concepts of reincarnation and your many lifetimes, both past and future. Ways to access your many lifetimes are provided, plus a list of benefits you will derive from your efforts.

Besides the cases and information on reincarnation, at the end of each chapter I have provided a creative meditation that relates directly to the information within the chapter. The intent of the creative meditations is to help you directly explore your many lifetimes as a way to empower your present lifetime.

There are several ways you can approach the meditations that are included in this book. First, you can read them to yourself, one line at a time. Be sure you comprehend the line as a complete thought before moving on to the next line. I like to read a line, then close my eyes and visualize what I have read. This takes a little longer, but the effort is well worth it. Second, you can have someone you trust read the meditations to you. Be sure to have this person read the meditation script slowly enough for you to comprehend and visualize the content. Have the person take plenty of time, pausing for a few moments between each line and between paragraphs. Third, you can tape record the meditations using your own voice and play it back to yourself. I suggest playing soft music in the background to enhance the recording and help you relax even more. When taping the meditation, make sure you won't be interrupted. Also, keep the noise level to a minimum to assure a good quality recording that you can listen to several times. If you do make a mistake when tape recording the script, merely stop the recorder, rewind the tape, and do it again correctly. You may get a clicking sound each time in the tape when you do this, so try to read the script through as much as possible. If you don't want to do the tape recording yourself, you can ask a family member or friend with a pleasant voice to read the meditation scripts for you into the recorder. If you decide to do this, make certain the person you select is someone you like and have positive feelings about. You are more likely to trust, relax, and absorb what is being said on the recording.

If you decide to proceed with a meditation alone, it may not be a bad idea to have a friend check on you about an hour after you start.

Be careful not to drive, use heavy machinery, or try to do other activities when reading or listening to the meditations. You need to focus your complete attention on the meditation itself. Plus, when you meditate, you enter a deeply relaxed state which is not conducive to activities such as driving, riding a bike, jogging, talking on the phone, working on the computer, working with machinery or appliances, and so forth.

The overall intent of this book is to share accounts about people experiencing other lifetimes, and at the same time, present a plausible argument for reincarnation. Our personal recollections of our past, present, and future life-time experiences provide a map for our soul's journey, and for living each and every lifetime to its fullest potential.

CHAPTER ONE

The Basics of Reincarnation

Souls never die, but always on quitting one abode pass to another. All things change, nothing perishes. The soul passes hither and thither, occupying now this body, now that, passing from the body of a beast into that of a man, and then into a beast's again. As a wax is stamped with certain figures, then melted, then stamped anew with others, yet it is always the same wax, so the soul, being always the same, yet wears at different times, different forms.

Pythagoras

—·—

I n his essay "The Evidence of Survival of Claimed Memories of Former Incarnations," Dr. Ian Stevenson writes about the case of a six-year-old Belgian boy named Robert, who would point to the portrait of his dead uncle Albert and tell his family members he was the person in the picture. At the age of three, without being taught, Robert dived into a swimming pool, emulating Albert, who had been an excellent diver. Robert also complained of clicking noises by saying, "Don't! Don't! They killed me that way the last time." Uncle Albert had died from machine-gun fire in 1915 during World War I while he was trying to destroy a German emplacement. Lastly, Robert's grandmother reported that the boy used all the pet names and had the same likes and dislikes that her son Albert had when he was alive.

Accounts of people such as Robert transcend all of our bounds of normal reality. Things like that don't normally happen. When they do, it causes a ripple that forces us to evaluate our belief systems. When you experience something extraordinary, it often expands your personal awareness and shifts your views of reality.

Statistics show that a substantial part of the population believes in some form of reincarnation. Not only that, but the numbers of people having past life experiences seems to be rising on a daily basis, even in the West, where the population is predominantly Christian, a spiritual tradition that doesn't particularly hold with reincarnation. In Christianity, you have one lifetime to prove yourself worthy of entering heaven and gaining communion with the divine. To me, that seems like an awful lot of pressure to put on a person in one lifetime.

A recent Gallup Poll shows that 23 percent of Americans believe in reincarnation, including 25 percent of the Catholics and 21 percent of the Protestants polled. Notable historical figures who believed in reincarnation include Benjamin Franklin, Henry Ford, and General George Patton.

Another of Stevenson's cases that he writes about in his book *Cases of the Reincarnation Type, Volume 1: India* involves a young Indian boy named Jagdish Chandra. Born in 1923, Jagdish at the age of three and a half began talking about a past life. He described being one of two sons of Babuji Pandey, who lived in a neighboring Indian state. Jagdish's father took the boy to the place Jagdish described as part of his past life. Through a labyrinth of streets, the boy found the Pandey house. The previous life had been one of a Brahman and the current life was one of a lesser caste. From birth, Jagdish had demanded that his food be prepared the Brahman way. He displayed many of the behavioral patterns of this previous life and knew many of his previous relatives.

The boy's claims of a past life checked out in scientific investigation. What gives this case credibility is the fact that the boy had the experiences from a very early age. His father had kept written accounts of the experiences from the beginning. The past life described was of someone who lived a distance away and was of a higher caste.

Unlike Christianity, Eastern spiritual traditions readily embrace the concept of reincarnation. Basically they say that the soul or spirit is imperishable. It is eternal and has a divinelike quality whose quest is to return "home." In Hinduism, this divine home is called moksha. In Buddhism, it is called nirvana.

Within Eastern traditions, reincarnation is the vehicle for getting home, for returning to the divine, to the one. You live multiple lifetimes in which you experience every facet of life, eventually bringing you enlightenment and oneness with the divine.

Throughout the world, reincarnation is portrayed in many ways, from the Caribou Inuit, who believe that the dead are brought back to life with the help of the moon to take the form of not only humans but also animals, to the Hawaiians, who believe reincarnation happens in stages that move from rocks to humans. The Egyptians perceived it as the immortal soul, and the Celts perceived it as rebirth. The Christians perceive it as resurrection. Ultimately these are all forms of reincarnation, a cross-cultural concept that is universal.

Dr. Arthur Guirdham in his book *The Cathars and Reincarnation* recounts how a woman had suffered since the age of twelve from nightmares of murder and massacre. During the course of her therapy, she told the therapist about her dreams and showed him writings she had done when she was a young girl. Some of the things she had written were verses of songs done in Medieval French, a language she had not studied. The language was connected with the Cathars, a religious group persecuted and burned at the stake in the Middle Ages for, among other things, their belief in reincarnation. A search of thirteenth-century manuscripts revealed she was accurate to the last detail in the information she wrote down. Besides that, four of the songs that she had written down were found in the archives.

The Immortal or Imperishable Soul

The Benu was a fabled yellow and red bird with green eyes that symbolized the rising and regenerating sun. Egyptian mythology tells us that every 500 years, the young bird comes to Heliopolis carrying a ball of myrrh. The ball contains the embalmed body of the bird's father, which is then buried in the temple of the sun. The Greeks call it the phoenix, a bird that builds its nest from twigs of cassia and frankincense in which to die. A worm then crawls out of the dead phoenix and is transformed into a new phoenix.

In another account, every 500 years the phoenix travels from its home in India to Heliopolis, carrying spices that are used to build an altar or pyre where the bird is burned. On the third day, the new phoenix rises from the ashes to live again for another 500 years.

The phoenix is a mythological motif, symbolizing the

immortal or imperishable soul that is eternally being rein-carnated, reborn, and resurrected back to life. Classical Greek historian Herodotus wrote that the Egyptians were the first to believe in an immortal soul.

In the Egyptian scheme of things, the gods left the earthly plane long ago, and those that were left behind were less than godly, who by being reincarnated in earthly form could once again rejoin the divine energy of their ancestors. This basic belief is echoed in the spiritual tradi-tions of the Greeks, Romans, and Celts.

The Natural Cycle of Rebirth

Mirroring the cycles of nature, these traditions believe the energy of the goddess is born in the spring, comes to fruition in the summer, fades in the autumn, and lies dor-mant through the winter, waiting to be reborn again in the spring. Everyone who enjoys gardening is familiar with the idea of rebirth.

Within earth-spirited traditions such as Wicca, the association is the same as in gardening. The cycles are continually being reborn in the spring. In addition, god-desses and gods have many incarnations or faces, giving the idea of reincarnation divine proportions.

The idea that the divine is reincarnated and eternal is everywhere throughout the world, and as aspects of the divine, living beings are also part of the immortal or imper-ishable soul. In terms of rebirth, the fact that the soul is born, dies, and is reborn is part of the procession of life.

This concept that nothing truly dies, but is continually being reborn, is a prominent aspect of the Greek story of Persephone. Hades, god of the underworld, was out perusing the Earth in his chariot when he came upon the beautiful Persephone, daughter of Demeter, goddess of the seasons and harvest. Hades immediately fell in love with Persephone and carried her off in his chariot to the underworld.

In time, Demeter went looking for her daughter. When she couldn't find her, she was told by someone who had seen the deed that her daughter had been taken by Hades. The goddess was stricken with grief over the loss of her daughter and as a result, the Earth experienced wintertime. It became rainy and cold and the crops couldn't grow.

Finally, the plea went out to Zeus to somehow end Demeter's depression so the world could live again. Zeus decreed that Persephone could come back to Earth as long as she hadn't eaten anything while in the kingdom of the dead. Fortunately, Persephone had not eaten anything because of her grief over being separated from her mother. When she was told by Hades that she could return to Earth, he also offered her a pomegranate, and in her joy at leaving, she ate six seeds. Because of this, Zeus decided that Persephone would live six months on Earth with her mother and the other six months of the year with Hades in the underworld.

This story offers an excellent mythological motif of rebirth and reincarnation. Each year the goddess's daughter is taken from her by the forces of death and in her grief she neglects the Earth, where everything dies or goes into a state of dormancy. Each year the goddess's daughter is brought back to life to once again join her mother, who in a feeling of joy brings life back to the Earth with the coming of spring. Overall, this story ties the divine together with the earthly in a union involving the eternal regeneration of both.

Reincarnation and Resurrection

The book of Job says, "I shall die in my nest, and I shall multiply my days as the phoenix." In the Christian context, the phoenix does not become reincarnated or reborn, but instead symbolizes the concept of resurrection. Akin to resuscitation, resurrection involves bringing a soul back to life in the same body that it once occupied. This contrasts with reincarnation in that the soul is not incarnated into a new physical body, but it compares to reincarnation in the sense that there is life after death, with the implication that even in its resurrected form, the soul is immortal.

In the early stages of Christianity, church fathers were influenced by classical Greeks such as Pythagoras and Plato, as well as the Hermetic writings, all of which supported the idea of reincarnation. Origen, a leading Christian theologian of the second and third centuries, taught that souls had existed in previous worlds and would be reborn again in future worlds. In 533 C.E., the second council of Constantinople decreed that reincarnation did not fit into church doctrines, and as such, was consigned to the underground of Christian thought.

Afterward, gnostic groups such as the Cathars continued to believe in reincarnation, in particular the Albigenses, who flourished in southern France before being brutally wiped out for believing in reincarnation. In the thirteenth century, reincarnation was finally decreed heresy by the Catholic Church.

An integral part of history and evolution revolves around the idea that religions borrow from earlier religions. For example, many of the Catholic saints such as Saint Bridget and Saint Anne are basically the same deities as those in Druid traditions. Because of their connections with the "old religions" such as the Druids, Catholics are more likely to entertain the idea of reincarnation than Protestants.

One Catholic who has been working with cases of past lives in his role as a hypnotherapist is Father Marty Patton, president of the International Medical and Dental Hypnotherapy Association. In one particular case he has posted on the Internet at *www.infinityinst.com*, he describes a woman who came to see him because she was angry all the time and her second marriage was faltering. He regressed her to a life in which she was a thirteen-year-old Jewish French girl when the Nazis first overran France in World War II. She and a group of other children were arrested and placed in a boxcar on a train to a concentration camp. During the trip, the boxcar had problems and was abandoned, with the children left to die slowly of starvation. The children called out to the townspeople, but no one helped them.

Regressions determined that the woman was angry because of the way she died, but by reliving the experience, she began to get some perspective on it. In the words of Patton,

> We started to review that lifetime of the angry 13-year-old and the people she saw in this life as teachers, religious people, authority figures and neighbors. Spiritually she had brought back with her three of the children who had died under her care. After we released these entities, she saw that she was living with people who were in that lifetime with her. Her first husband was one of the guards that left the boxcar on the siding. Two of her children were under her care on the train, and her present husband was one of the townspeople who failed to assist. She realized that she was working out the trauma of that death; her second husband was trying to make up for his lack of courage in that previous lifetime; and her children chose her to protect them in this lifetime. Her anger subsided. She changed immediately, so much so that she was elected to head a children's Christmas charity. She became a strong Christian lady who loved her neighbors. And, most importantly, she was no longer angry.

Indications from recent polls and surveys suggest that more than two-thirds of the people worldwide believe in reincarnation, and the numbers continue to grow at a steady rate. As more people have experiences and more research is done, reincarnation starts to move from the realm of the unbelievable to the realm of the probable. This is particularly true for baby boomers, such as myself, as we reach that point in our lives when we start thinking about our own mortality, and what that means in terms of the whole of our lifetime. Many of us feel that what we avoided in this lifetime may come back around in future lifetimes.

Many people wonder if our life force continues after we die, a question that can conclusively be answered only when we die. Beyond that, it's speculative. At the same time, the number of accounts from people detailing other lifetimes continues to grow at tremendous rates. In addition, researchers are using more scientific methods to check out these accounts. Age-old spiritual ideas regarding the immortal soul are meeting up with the new scientific techniques of the twenty-first century, and becoming like two streams flowing into one.

What Is Reincarnation?

One of the earliest and most well-known accounts of reincarnation was in 1824, when a nine-year-old boy named Katsugoro, the son of a Japanese farmer, told his sister about a past life. The boy had vivid remembrances of a life in which he was the son of another farmer in another village, and had died from the effects of smallpox in 1810. Katsugoro could remember dozens of specific events about his past life, including details about his family and the village where they lived, even though he had never been there. He even remembered the time of his death, his burial, and the time he spent before being reborn. The facts he related were subsequently verified by an investigation.

A simple analogy for reincarnation can be found in each day of your life. In the morning a new day is born and you wake up, ready to live again. You begin by making out a mental list of things that you would like to accomplish that day. After doing your morning activities, you go to work, where most of your day is usually spent. In the evening, you come home from work and live out the last hours of your day, engaging in activities you like to do, being with family and friends, relaxing, and coming to terms with your day and who you are. At night before going to bed, you might evaluate all the things you did and didn't do, making a mental list of the things you need to do tomorrow. As you retire for the evening, you again become one with the night, drifting into a dream state. This period represents the in-between period, between lives. The last thing you are thinking about as you move into a state of sleep is often reflected in your first thought the next morning.

Let's take this analogy further. If each day you are reincarnated into a new lifetime, where you experience things, that could be considered a micro-lifetime. If each day or micro-lifetime is put together into the whole of your lifetime, it becomes a macro-lifetime. Ideally, the purposes of the micro-lifetimes move you along to the essential purpose of the macro-lifetime.

As a whole, reincarnation presupposes several basic ideas, including the notion that living things survive death in an energetic form, and that this energy reincarnates in physical form. The following four concepts offer a basic definition of reincarnation:

1. *Each person has a soul/spirit.*
2. *This soul/spirit survives the death of the physical body by going to an in-between place.*
3. *The soul/spirit is reborn into a new physical body.*
4. *The life and rebirth cycle evolves, possibly evolving into a divine state of being.*

One of the strongest cases for reincarnation comes from researchers at the University of Virginia. The case involves a boy from Sri Lanka named Sujith. When he was a young child and barely able to speak, he started talking about a previous life. The life was as a man named Sammy, who had lived in the village of Gorakana. The village was eight miles to the south of Sujith's home. Sujith relayed the events of his life as Sammy, including his occupation as a railroad worker and sideline as a dealer of a bootleg whiskey called arrack. The boy went on to describe how Sammy one day had an argument with his wife, Maggie. Storming out of the house, he went out and got drunk, and later on while walking along a highway, he was struck by a truck and died.

Sujith as a young boy often asked to be taken to Gorkana, although his family had never been there. The boy also had a fondness for cigarettes and arrack, just as

Sammy had when he was alive. One of the researchers, a professor of psychiatry from the University of Virginia, investigated the details of Sujith's description of his life as Sammy, and found that a man by the name of Sammy Fernando had indeed died six months before Sujith's birth, just as the boy had said. When they checked things out, investigators confirmed more than sixty details in Sujith's life as Sammy. Later on, when introduced to Sammy's family, Sujith astonished them with his personal knowledge of them, including their pet names.

Stories about previous lives and reincarnation have existed for many years, especially in Eastern cultures in which reincarnation is an integral part of their spirituality. What is different in terms of current reincarnation studies is that these stories and accounts are being checked out and verified for accuracy. As more of these cases check out and become published, it becomes more apparent that either reincarnation, or something that is beyond the normal scope of things, is occurring.

The Cosmic Database

The people having these experiences are obviously tapping into something beyond ordinary reality. Also, the fact that these experiences can be verified by scientific investigation proves that these experiences have "realness" to them in terms of the physical world. Where are these experiences coming from? Is it reincarnation? Some suggest that these experiences come from people tapping into a giant universal database, somewhat akin to the Internet.

Carl Jung proposed the idea that reincarnation is an archetype and operating mechanism in the collective unconsciousness. In other words, the belief that you are reincarnated is part of your basic psyche. When you tap into the collective unconsciousness, you perceive it as a previous life. What you are actually tapping into is the giant database that holds every thought and action through all time. What you perceive is based on which keys you tap into.

Edgar Cayce, "The Sleeping Prophet," as he is often called, was a devout Christian who at first did not believe in reincarnation. But as a "medical intuitive" who looked for the spiritual causes of his patients' illnesses, he kept running headlong into the concept of reincarnation. At first he resisted the idea, but later on it became an integral part of his "readings" for people who came to him for help.

When Cayce did readings, he tapped into a cosmic database that he called the Akashic Records. Much like Jung's collective unconsciousness, the Akashic Records form a universal book of life that is imprinted with the energy of everything within oneness. The implications of tapping into this divine database are infinite. The idea is to get the human out of the way so that the information flows freely through you.

Cayce used a particular technique to tap into the Akashic Records. This technique involved seeing yourself as a tiny dot outside of your being. You feel oppressed and lonely within the darkness. You become conscious of a beam of white light as it pierces the darkness around you. You move upward, following the white light until you reach the place you want to be. When you reach this point, all information is waiting to be accessed, and you become a conduit for the divine, and true enlightenment is possible. One lifetime is a candle, whereas multiple lifetimes are a sun to light the way on your path to oneness.

Why do people connect to certain past lives? Connections are being drawn that move in particular ways. As with everything, choices are made that affect lifetimes both in the physical and energetic realms. As a human being, you are both physical and energetic. The idea that you would gravitate between the two is, in a way, the essence of reincarnation. You move from the energetic to the physical and back to the energetic, much like the cycles of the phoenix. Once again, the pattern seems to replicate itself, much like your DNA structure plays an important part in how your offspring turn out, particularly on a physical level.

The idea of reincarnation unfolds many layers of con-current thought patterns. You move from the energetic into the physical, transforming the spirit into a soul and giving it a physical body. The concepts of the soul and the spirit are at times thought to be similar, but they are different in some ways.

Soul and Spirit

The case of Victor Vincent, a Tlingit Indian from Alaska, is documented in Ian Stevenson's book *Twenty Cases Suggestive of Reincarnation*. Before he died, Vincent told his niece Corliss Chotkin that he would come back to life as her son, and would have two birthmarks, one on his nose and one on his back, that corresponded to marks Vincent had on his body.

Eighteen months after Vincent died, Chotkin did indeed have a son who was born with birthmarks on his nose and back, just as Vincent had described. At an early age, the child called out to his mother, "Don't you know me? I'm Kahkody," which was Vincent's tribal name. In addition the child recognized people and described events from Vincent's life without prompting. Vincent's tendency to stutter and his interest in fixing boat engines also manifested themselves later in Chotkin's son.

The incorrect translation of the original Hebrew texts leads many to believe that "soul" and "spirit" are the same, but they are not. The problem arose from the very first translation of the Hebrew texts into Greek. At that time, the Greek language lacked different terms to describe "nephesh" (the Hebrew word for soul) and "rowah" (spirit). Therefore the translators of the Septuagint used the same word, "psyche," to describe both terms, even though they were different.

Soul and spirit are intangible and intricately tied to each other. The soul is the life force that animates a person, and when it is no longer present, the person is dead. The spirit is a person's energetic pattern that transcends three-dimensional reality and connects the individual to the divine. As a consequence, soul is thought of more in terms of self and specific character, whereas spirit is perceived as energy and the holistic pattern.

Some African and South American cultures describe the soul as a small flying thing that during sleep and at the time of death flies from the mouth in the form of a butterfly, insect, or bird. This metaphor implies that the soul is attached to the individual being, but that this attachment applies only when the person is in a conscious state.

Within Eastern traditions, Hinduism believes in the existence of a soul, which they call the "atman." The soul is reincarnated through lifetimes. In contrast, Buddhism says that the personal entity or soul is not reincarnated. Only the "annatta," containing the characteristics, dispositions, and tendencies, carries forth. In some ways the annatta is more akin to spirit than soul. In this perception, it is spirit that is reincarnated rather than soul.

To carry it further, spirit is eternal and reincarnates into lifetimes, generating souls that connect into the overall spirit of who you are over multiple lifetimes. You exist in this lifetime and all other lifetimes at the same time because the timeless aspect of spirit links them all together in the interconnected fabric of oneness. The spirit incarnates into an energetic soul that is then born into a physical body. This is the basic process of reincarnation.

How Reincarnation Works

Another case documented by Stevenson can be found in Tom Shroder's book "A Matter of Death and Life." The case involves a middle-class Druze girl living in Beirut named Suzanne, who at the age of sixteen months, picked up the phone and said, "Hello, Leila?" repeatedly into the receiver.

Soon after, Suzanne told her parents that she was Leila's mother, and by the time she was two, she gave the names of all her children, her husband, parents, and brothers in that lifetime. After begging her parents to take her to her "real" home, the parents began asking around and eventually found a family that fit Suzanne's descriptions.

After contacting the family, they found out that the woman Suzanne remembered being had died while undergoing heart surgery in Richmond, Virginia. Before going into surgery, she had tried desperately to call her daughter Leila. Discussion with the family revealed that many of the details Suzanne had given about her past life as this woman were accurate, including names and places. She correctly identified photographs of her family in her former life as this woman. The meeting of Suzanne with her former family had an unnerving effect on them because of the accuracy of what she said and her interaction with each of them.

The study of past lives has become an integral part of the study of reincarnation. This is because a lot of people seem to have past life experiences and many have been verified.

Primarily, the two ways that past lives have been studied is through past life regressions using hypnosis and through people who are spontaneously reliving past life experiences. In spontaneous experiences, there is no prompting and they usually begin surfacing in early childhood.

Hypnotherapy has become an invaluable tool for

modern psychologists as well as for medical doctors and dentists. By regressing people to traumatic events in their lives, psychologists and hynotherapists can help move them beyond some problems. Early on in the practice of hypnotherapy, patients began regressing beyond childhood, into past lives. These revelations were often awe inspiring to the therapists, who were rapidly moving into unknown territory. The experiences were too "real" to be ignored, so some of the therapists began researching and verifying them.

Since then, hypnotherapy has continued to be useful in the exploration, treatment, and research of past lives. Therapists such as Helen Walmbach and Carol Bowman have shown that helping patients move through past life experiences has medical value in that the patients improve both mentally and physically. Past life regression has thera-peutic value when the patient relives the experience of a past life and in so doing is healed of phobias or physical ailments.

Stevenson's approach to past lives and reincarnation is perhaps the least tainted because he investigates only cases in which revisiting the past life experience is sponta-neous and not initiated in any way. In many of his cases, children start talking of past lives, and their accounts through time become vivid with detail. This is what Stevenson likes because he checks out each one of the details in the past life experience. Also, rather than "past life," he calls it a "previous personality."

The Great Balancer

Karma has often been labeled "the great balancer" in that people often perceive it as a force that rewards good behavior and actions with "good karma" and bad behavior and actions with "bad karma." In terms of reincarnation, karma whether good or bad is carried over into other lifetimes. In particular bad karma can be atoned for and balanced in future lifetimes, just as many things that happen to people in their present lifetime can be attributed to the influences of past lives. The common perception is that if someone did something bad to you in a past life, they come back in this life or a future life and make amends to you.

In a more practical sense, karma infers that every action you take produces a dynamic result that affects other beings, often in a myriad of ways. An analogy for this would be throwing a stone into a pool of water. As the stone hits, it creates a splash, depending on its size and speed. Beyond that, the action of the stone being thrown into the water begins a series of ripples. These ripples move outward from the point of impact, and again depending on size and speed, affect everything around them.

In terms of the new physics as postulated by physicists such as Dr. David Bohm, everything is made up of energy. Much like the water in the example, every action produces a rippling effect that moves through infinite realms of existence, leaving open the possibility of affecting many other people's lives in an infinite number of ways.

In addition, karma has an evolutionary quality to it, in that as you live multiple lifetimes, you move or progress toward some kind of spiritual goal. In most spiritual traditions that goal is a joining or oneness with the divine, regardless of its name. Everything in life progresses from one point to another. Whether this progress is actually forward movement is fodder for philosophical debate. Nonetheless, all life has a dynamic element to it that progresses from point A to point B and then onward, and then often back around. Karma is the dynamic force that keeps the universe essentially in a state of motion. In Eastern spiritual traditions, that motion is spread out over multiple lifetimes, where karma is the "cause" and becoming one with the divine is the "effect."

Much like those ripples in the pool of water, time is circular so that past lives and future lives become one and the same. Because from your perspective you live one life, from birth, through childhood, through adulthood, until you get old and die, you see life as moving in essentially a straight line. Instead time is curved, much in the same way that Albert Einstein said space is curved, and not linear as earlier scientists had presupposed.

The idea of future lifetimes is a logical next step in the study of reincarnation. If you have past lives and a present life, then you must in time have future lives—that is of course unless you've already reached a state of divinity, at which point your mission has achieved its apex and you no longer need to reincarnate in earthly form.

In two-dimensional reality, past lives represent where

you have been, and future lives represent where you are going. From the perspective of your present life, representing where you are "now" is how you normally view the whole of your past and future lives.

How Reincarnation Affects Your Life

The reputable cases for reincarnation continue to increase as more research is done on the phenomena. Shroder discuses some of Stevenson's more convincing cases in his book "A Matter of Death and Life."

(In one case, a boy recalled a life as a twenty-five-year-old mechanic, who died when he was thrown from a speeding car. The boy recited all the specifics of his death, including who was driving the car and where the car crashed, all of which was later verified.

(In another case, a girl recalled a past life as a teenager named Sheila, who remembered the town she lived in as well as her parents and brothers and sisters, and that she died while crossing the road. When Sheila's family met the girl, they were astonished when she recognized them by name and relationship without prompting.

(In yet another case, a boy in Virginia named Joseph called his grandmother "mom" and his mother by her given name. While growing up the boy began recalling obscure events from his life as Uncle David, a relative who had died twenty years earlier but was never spoken about by the family.

Knowledge of past lives and future lives can shed light on your talents, preferences, aversions, and strengths, sometimes in surprising ways. If you are creative in some way, possibly you developed your skill over many lifetimes of training and practice. Delving into past lives can uncover talents you didn't know you had or reasons for the inclinations you already have. Most likely your strongest friendships today began long before you were physically born into this lifetime.

You as a living being have a mission in life. This mission is most likely imprinted in your DNA coding, besides being recorded in the Akashic Records and "collective unconscious." Everything you do is imprinted with your patterns, much like the concept of fingerprints. You have an energetic pattern that sets you apart as distinct from all other living beings. The idea of a mission gives the pattern focus and thrusts forward to the heart of your personal evolution.

Reincarnation is at its essence about the dynamic element in life that continually moves you and everything else forward. Working with this dynamic element is the key to successful living. If you struggle with it, you feel as though you are stuck in the muck and mire, and if you flow with it, you feel as though you are floating on a cloud.

In this lifetime you have a calling, a life mission. By becoming attuned with your calling, with your mission, you can heal present ailments and move yourself along the evolutionary trail. You move beyond your physical body to what is really going on spiritually, beyond three-dimensional reality, to the great beyond.

By becoming aware of your past, present, and future lives, you can better understand who you are now. Understanding that, you know what course to take, both to move you forward in this life and as an overall being on the road to "enlightenment." The "eternal now" is a filter for the past, present, and future. Staying in the moment, in the now, is an essential part of the whole experience.

Within the silence of the soul is a voice that calls upon the winds of oneness. By stilling the chatter in your mind, you can tap into a force or energy that moves you into the past and the future. Becoming aware of the layers of reincarnation helps you move through that which holds you back so you can move forward as a multidimensional being of energy.

From the present, the past, the future, or the karmic, you are who you are—a distinct signature upon the whole of oneness. This serves to guide you on the road to discovering what that signature is. In the immortal words of my writing muse, Jake the boogie-woogie bullfrog, "And so the adventure begins."

Guided Breathwork Meditation

Each chapter of this book includes a guided meditation. These meditations are intended to clarify the concept of reincarnation. They can be used to help you integrate the various elements of reincarnation so you can apply them as you so choose.

You can tape-record the following Guided Breathwork Meditation in your own voice or, if you prefer, have your partner or a friend slowly read the meditation to you. Or you can read it to yourself, following along a paragraph at a time. (See pages 4 and 5 for tips on reading the meditations.)

Before doing the meditation, I suggest that you switch on your phone's answering machine, turn down the volume, and turn off the ringer—or unplug your phone. Tell your family or roommates that you don't want to be disturbed for about thirty minutes. Put the dog, cat, other pets, and your cell phone out of the room to avoid interruptions while you meditate.

Meditation

SIT OR RECLINE COMFORTABLY. LOOSEN ANY CLOTHING, BELTS, OR SHOES THAT MIGHT BE BINDING YOU. JUST GET AS COMFORTABLE AS YOU CAN. UNCROSS YOUR ARMS AND LEGS AND TAKE A FEW DEEP BREATHS, SETTLING AND SINKING INTO THE SURFACE BENEATH YOU A LITTLE BIT MORE WITH EACH BREATH.

NOW TAKE A DEEP BREATH THROUGH YOUR MOUTH, HOLD IT FOR THREE COUNTS, AND THEN EXHALE THROUGH YOUR NOSE FOR THREE COUNTS. BEGIN TO FEEL A WARM WHITE LIGHT SURROUNDING YOUR ENTIRE BODY AND FILLING YOUR HEAD. AS YOU DO THIS, RELAX YOUR FOREHEAD AND THE MUSCLES AROUND YOUR EYES.

Take another deep breath through your mouth, hold it for three counts, and then exhale through your nose for three counts. As you do this, feel the warm white light flow over and relax the muscles inside and outside of your mouth. Let go of any tension in your mouth and tongue and relax your jaw, just allowing it to soften and drop.

Take another breath through your mouth, hold it for three counts, and then exhale through your nose for three counts. As you exhale feel the warm white light fill and relax the muscles of your neck, shoulders, arms, hands, and fingers, and flow into your fingertips.

Continue breathing through your mouth and exhaling out your nose, imagining the warm white light filling and relaxing the muscles of your chest and stomach, flowing through and relaxing your upper, middle, and lower back.

Take another breath through your mouth, and exhale through your nose, filling your buttocks, thighs, calves, ankles, heels, feet, and toes with warm white light.

Your entire body is filled with warm white light, completely relaxed, yet aware of every detail of your experience.

Now begin to imagine yourself walking in

A MOUNTAIN MEADOW ON A LAZY, WARM SUMMER AFTERNOON. THE SKY IS A DEEP AZURE BLUE AND THE SUN FILTERS THROUGH THE OAK TREES AROUND YOU. AS YOU WANDER SLOWLY ALONG A PATH IN THE MEADOW, YOU ARE SURROUNDED BY JEWEL-LIKE WILDFLOWERS OF EVERY COLOR. YOU CAN SMELL THE GRASS AND FLOWERS ON THE SOFT WIND. THE FLOWERS AND GRASS BLEND TOGETHER INTO A FRAGRANT, CALMING SCENT THAT PUTS YOU AT EASE.

YOU CAN HEAR BLUEJAYS CAWING IN THE CANOPY OF THE OAK TREES AND THE SOUND OF RUNNING WATER NEARBY. YOU CAN SMELL THE WATER ON THE SOOTHING WIND. INSECTS BUZZ HERE AND THERE, AND GRAY SQUIRRELS SCURRY UP THE OAK TREES NOW AND AGAIN. YOU SEE A DEER BOLT AND RUN THROUGH THE MEADOW.

DIRECTLY IN FRONT OF YOU, YOU SEE A BEAUTI-FUL FULL-LENGTH MIRROR. AS YOU WALK OVER TO IT, YOU CAN SEE THE FACES OF HUNDREDS OF PEOPLE CARVED IN ITS WOODEN FRAME. IT'S A MAGIC MIRROR WITH NO VISIBLE SUPPORT AS YOU LOOK AT IT MORE CLOSELY. IT IS A MIRROR THAT CAN SHOW YOU MAGI-CAL IMAGES. YOU STAND IN FRONT OF THE MIRROR AND LOOK INTO IT.

AS YOU GAZE INTO THE LOOKING GLASS, YOU SEE YOURSELF HEALTHY AND STRONG. YOUR SKIN IS GLOWING WITH HEALTH AND YOUR EYES ARE BRIGHT AND RADIANT. YOUR BODY IS FLEXIBLE AND STRONG AND YOU LOOK FIT AND TERRIFIC. YOU SEE THE

EXPRESSION ON YOUR FACE IN THE MIRROR AND NOTICE THAT YOU LOOK HAPPY AND JOYFUL, AWARE AND RELAXED.

YOU LOOK AWAY FROM THE MAGIC MIRROR, TURN, AND WALK SLOWLY ALONG THE MEADOW PATH UNTIL YOU COME TO A SMALL MOUNTAIN CREEK. THERE ARE STONES OF EVERY COLOR AND SIZE IN THE CREEK BED, AND YOU BEND DOWN AND PICK UP A SMALL WHITE ONE. THE WATER IS COLD AND REFRESHING ON YOUR HAND AND FINGERTIPS. YOU FEEL THE WHITE STONE BETWEEN YOUR FINGERS AND THEN GENTLY TOSS IT BACK INTO THE CREEK AS YOU MAKE A SILENT WISH TO THE DIVINE.

YOU CONTINUE ALONG THE PATH AS IT WINDS ALONG THE CREEK BANK, AND YOU COME TO A MAG-NIFICENT OAK TREE, MUCH LARGER AND WIDER THAN ANY OTHER OAK YOU HAVE EVER SEEN. YOU SEE A NATURAL OVAL DOORWAY, LIKE A HUGE TREE KNOT, EMBEDDED IN THE TRUNK OF THE MAGNIFICENT OAK, AND YOU WALK OVER TO IT.

AS YOU KNOCK THREE TIMES ON THE OVAL DOOR, IT OPENS BY ITSELF, AND YOU EASILY AND EFFORTLESSLY ENTER THE INTERIOR OF THE TREE. ONCE INSIDE, YOU REALIZE THAT THE TREE IS A KIND OF ARCHIVE, FILLED WITH SCROLLS UPON SCROLLS WITH NAMES ON THEM.

THE INTERIOR OF THE TREE IS GIGANTIC, AND IT IS BATHED IN A SOFT WHITE LIGHT. A BEAUTIFUL WOMAN DRESSED IN FLOWING WHITE ROBES COMES

OVER TO WHERE YOU ARE STANDING. SHE IS LIKE A GODDESS, LOVELY AND WISE. SHE TAKES YOU GENTLY BY THE HAND AND LEADS YOU DEEPER INTO THE INTERIOR OF THE TREE LIBRARY. EVERYWHERE YOU LOOK, YOU SEE SCROLLS WITH NAMES ON THEM.

THE WOMAN IN WHITE LEADS YOU OVER TO ONE AREA IN THE LIBRARY. SHE BECKONS YOU TO ASCEND A NATURAL LADDER MADE OF TREE BRANCHES. AS YOU EFFORTLESSLY CLIMB UP THE STURDY LADDER OF BRANCHES, YOU BEGIN TO LOOK AT THE SCROLLS. SUDDENLY YOU SEE YOUR NAME ENGRAVED IN GOLD ON THE END OF ONE VERY SPECIAL SCROLL.

YOU TAKE THIS SCROLL OUT OF ITS RESTING PLACE AND GO DOWN THE LADDER. YOU UNROLL THE SCROLL AND READ THE FOLLOWING MESSAGE: "YOU ARE ENERGY. YOU ARE SPIRIT. YOU ARE ONE. YOU ARE CONNECTED DURING YOUR LIFETIME TO YOUR BODY. YOUR BODY IS THE EARTHLY VESSEL, THE HOME OF YOUR ENERGY AND SPIRIT."

YOU CONTINUE READING: "YOUR LIFETIMES ARE MIRRORS FOR YOU TO LOOK INTO AND SEE FACES OF YOURSELF. ALWAYS REMEMBER TO BEGIN, FILL, AND END EACH MOMENT WITH LOVE. BE FRIENDLY RATHER THAN HOSTILE. BE KIND RATHER THAN CRUEL. FILL YOUR HEART WITH LOVE AND SHARE THE LOVE IN YOUR HEART WITH THOSE YOU LOVE. CARRY LOVE AND RESPECT FOR YOURSELF AND OTHERS IN YOUR HEART."

YOU ROLL UP THE SCROLL, ASCEND THE LADDER, AND PUT THE SCROLL BACK INTO ITS RESTING PLACE.

You descend the ladder. The woman in white takes your hand and leads you back to the oval doorway. She speaks to you in words only you can hear. Listen to her simple message for a moment or two. It is for your ears only.

After you have heard the woman's message, thank her and bid her farewell. Then knock on the oval door three times. As the woman in white bids you farewell, the door opens and you step through it, and find yourself back outside the magnificent tree library.

As you walk back through the woods, you can hear the bluejays cawing and the creek water running. You follow the path along the creek bank and then back to the grassy meadow. You can feel the warm afternoon sun shining on your face and arms as you walk along. The scents of the flowers relax and calm you even more as you walk back into the meadow.

You walk over to the magic mirror and look at your reflection. You see yourself exactly as you are—a radiant loving being of light. You see yourself just the way you want to be, doing exactly what you want to be doing. Be there for a few moments. Immerse yourself in the joy of your reflection in the magic mirror. Smile at your reflection, and then look away.

NOW IN YOUR MIND'S EYE, WALK OVER TO ONE OF THE OAK TREES AT THE EDGE OF THE CLEARING. IMAGINE PUTTING YOUR HANDS ON THE BARK OF THE OAK TREE AND LEANING AGAINST THE TRUNK WITH YOUR BODY. LET THE TREE SUPPORT YOU AS MUCH AS POSSIBLE.

FEEL THE LIFE ENERGY OF THE TREE, THE LIFE ENERGY OF THE MEADOW AROUND YOU. ALLOW IT TO FILL YOU. SENSE THE ENERGY OF THE WILD-FLOWERS, MEADOW GRASS, BLUEJAYS, INSECTS, AND THE FLOWING SWIFTNESS OF THE MOUNTAIN CREEK. ALLOW THIS ENERGY TO ALSO FILL YOU. BREATHE IT IN. BECOME AWARE OF THE DIVINE SPIRIT IN EVERY THING AROUND YOU, ABSOLUTELY EVERY THING, INCLUDING YOURSELF. ALLOW THIS KNOWLEDGE TO FILL YOUR HEART WITH JOY AND GLADNESS. BREATHE IT IN.

NOW AS YOU FEEL THE BARK OF THE TREE AGAINST YOUR HANDS AND BODY, FEEL YOURSELF BECOMING VERY ALERT AND HIGHLY REFRESHED. BREATHE IN THROUGH YOUR MOUTH, HOLD YOUR BREATH FOR THREE COUNTS, AND THEN EXHALE THROUGH YOUR NOSE. DO THIS AT LEAST THREE TIMES, EACH TIME BREATHING IN WARM WHITE LIGHT AND BRIGHT ENERGY INTO YOUR ENTIRE BEING, FROM YOUR HEAD TO YOUR TOES. FEEL THE WARM WHITE LIGHT REFRESH AND REVITALIZE YOU. DO THIS FOR A FEW MOMENTS.

FEELING STRONG, RADIANT, AND FULL OF RELAX-

ING ENERGY, TAKE A DEEP BREATH THROUGH YOUR
MOUTH, AND EXHALE THROUGH YOUR NOSE. SLOWLY
OPEN YOUR EYES AND COME BACK TO YOUR WAKING
CONSCIOUSNESS, MOVING YOUR HANDS AND FEET,
WIGGLING YOUR TOES AND FINGERS. NOW COME
COMPLETELY BACK TO THE PRESENT MOMENT BY
CLAPPING YOUR HANDS TOGETHER THREE TIMES.

☛ *Take a few minutes to make any notes about the meditation experience that might be helpful to you. Write down how you felt before and after, as well as the benefits you derived from it.*

CHAPTER TWO
Past
Lives

I have been here before, but when or how I
cannot tell:
I know the grass beyond the door,
The sweet keen smell, the sighing sound, the
lights around the shore.
You have been mine before—How long ago I
may not know:
But just when at that swallow's soar, your
neck turned so,
Some veil did fall, I knew it all of yore.

Dante Gabriel Rossetti

What Are Past Lives?

In the book *The Children That Time Forgot* by Peter and Mary Harrison is the story of Nicola. On her second birthday, Nicola received a toy dog from her parents. The little girl told her mother that the toy reminded her of Muff, the dog she had had before. Because Nicola had never had a dog named Muff, her mother dismissed the episode as fantasy. A short time later, the girl asked why she wasn't a boy this time, like last time, when Mrs. Benson was her mother and Muff was her dog. Nicola went on describe a life in which people wore Victorian dress and she lived in a house next to railroad tracks in the town of Haworth in Yorkshire, England.

Curious, her mother took Nicola to Haworth, and the girl responded by going to the house she described in her past life experience. The house was as she had described, all the way to the railroad tracks. Upon investigation of the town records, the mother found that in 1875, a family named Benson lived in the town, and that they had a young son, who died when he was about six. Neither Nicola nor her mother had ever been to Haworth before. The question becomes, Did young Nicola actually have a past life as she described?

When talking about past lives, two important questions arise: (1) Does the soul or spirit of a particular person remain intact after the death of the physical body? and (2) Can this soul or spirit then be reborn into another physical body? These are the two essential questions that are usually asked when talking about reincarnation.

Traditional psychology answers "No" to both questions. It says that we are born, experience life, and then die. We do not come back in another body. Clinical psychologists maintain that past life experiences are the manifestations of our unconscious trying to express our repressed spiritual quests. We are asking to be acknowledged as a person. In other words, past lives are fantasies created by our unconscious to get attention. But this traditional view has fallen short of practical reality time and time again.

Trained Freudian psychologist Dr. Edith Fiore discusses past lives in her book *You Have Been Here Before*. She was treating one of her patients for sexual inhibitions that were causing him debilitating problems. After putting the patient under hypnosis, she began gradually regressing him back in age, to the time when the problem began. When she gave him the final suggestion to return to the source of the problem, he responded, "Two or three lifetimes ago I was a Catholic priest." He further described his past life as a seventeenth-century Italian priest.

Not a believer in past lives, Fiore dismissed it as a fantasy of the patient's subconscious. But soon after, the patient returned to confide in the doctor that his sexual problem was healed, and that on the whole, he felt much better about himself.

Being a traditionally trained psychologist, Fiore attempted to dismiss this case, but in her practice other accounts of past life experiences kept recurring, until she could no longer ignore them. In her work she discovered that not only did past life experiences affect her patients' ailments, both physical and mental, but also the conditions surrounding their death in the past life. These ailments ranged from migraine headaches and stomach disorders to debilitating fears and phobias.

One of Fiore's patients was a successful businessman who was so afraid of heights that he would never travel by airplane. He avoided going up in high buildings and driving over mountains. His fears were impinging on his career. After exhausting normal techniques, Fiore regressed the man to a past life in which he was a workman fixing a tile on a European church. He slipped from the roof, and as he was falling, was able to grab the gutter. Unfortunately, he was not able to hang on and fell to his death on the scaffolding below. After working through this past life experience, the patient was free of his crippling fear of heights.

Two things stand out from reliving past life experiences. First, these events are very real to the people experiencing them. Second, because of their realness, past life experiences can have profound healing effects on the person recalling the experience. These are things that traditional psychology can't explain and would like to ignore, even though the results are real, here, now, in this life.

Without a way to measure whether a person's spirit remains together after death and is then reborn into another body, the question of past lives may never be truly answered in a scientific sense. Meanwhile researchers of past lives are accumulating a great body of evidence suggesting that past lives are real, at least on some level of perception.

The Evidence
for Past Lives

As head of the Department of Psychiatry at the University
of Virginia School of Medicine, Dr. Ian Stevenson research-
es and verifies cases of past lives, including names and
dates. Unless the details surrounding the past life can be
proven and a person's past life descriptions match written
records of a deceased person, he does not consider the
case solved. In all, Stevenson has investigated more than
26,000 cases in his role as a past life detective.

In 1948, Swarnlata Mishra was born in India, and by
the age of three was recounting to her parents a life she
had lived as Biya Pathak, a woman who lived in a town
more than 100 miles away and had died in 1939 from a
pain in her throat. Stevenson found out about the case
from an Indian colleague who, when investigating the case,
went to the place Swarnlata had described. With her
description, he found the place without any problems.

The place belonged to the wealthy Pathak family.
After hearing the account from the researcher, Biya's husband, eldest brother, one of her sons, and nine townspeople
went to visit Swarnlata. She went around the room correctly identifying each of her relatives, and even called her
brother by his pet name, Babu. Even when her son, Murli,
attempted to mislead her and tell her that he was someone
else and that her son was really one of the townspeople,
she responded correctly and insisted Murli was her son.
Upon visiting the Pathak house, she correctly identified
more than two dozen people that Biya had known, address-

ing them by name and giving details of her life as Biya that were extremely accurate, even under rigorous scrutiny. Swarnlata gave more than fifty facts about her life as Biya that Stevenson personally verified.

In another account, three-year-old Michael Wright of Texas surprised his mother by describing in detail a past life, including his death in a fatal automobile crash. Even more surprising was that the past life he remembered was that of his mother's teenage boyfriend, who died in an accident just as Michael had described. No one in the family ever talked about the incident. The many stories just like Michael's point to something more than what we've been taught to believe in terms of traditional psychology.

Stevenson's research involves past life cases that come about spontaneously, without any aid. There are a surprisingly large number of these experiences. The research usually begins when a child begins discussing a past life.

The Role
of Modern Hypnotherapy

Another way to explore past lives is by using hypnotherapy. This useful technique is extremely effective in past life regression and continues to gain credibility in modern psychotherapy.

In 1952, therapist Morey Bernstein was conducting a hypnosis session with his patient Virginia Tighe, when suddenly she began to describe her past life as Bridget Murphy, a nineteenth-century Irishwoman who went by the nickname Bridey. In six different sessions, Tighe described in detail her birth in 1798, her childhood growing up around Cork, Ireland, her marriage to Sean Brian Joseph McCarthy, and her eventual death in 1858.

With the release of both a book and movie on the subject, the case of Bridey Murphy became one of the most famous cases of past lives. Because of poor record keeping in nineteenth-century Ireland, the case was never fully proved or disproved, at least not in the same way as Stevenson's cases. Bridey Murphy's case is important because it was one of the first cases in which hypnotherapy played a role in bringing about memories of a past life experience, albeit unintentionally.

Although the origins of hypnosis can be traced to Egypt and Greece, Friedrich Anton Mesmer, an Austrian born in 1773, is considered the father of modern hypnosis. Mesmer was known for placing magnets around the body in a technique he called animal magnetism. This practice is similar to the magnet body wraps used in healing therapies today. Mesmer would then pass his healing hands over patients, inducing them into trances that were relaxing and positive. One of his students, Marquis Armand de Puysequr, identified these mesmerizing, trancelike states as hypnosis.

In terms of modern hypnotherapy, one of the most influential people has been Milton K. Erickson, who as a child had a severe case of polio that was diagnosed as terminal. After proving the doctor wrong, Erickson went on to gain degrees in both medicine and psychology. In his practice as a psychiatrist, he learned to use stories, jokes, and practical advice as a means to move patients into a relaxed, life-changing state. With the comforting words, "My voice will be with you wherever you go," Erickson led the way in formulating techniques that are now used routinely in modern hypnotherapy.

Hypnosis alters a person's state of consciousness. It creates a very relaxed, calm state of mind in which the unconscious can be assessed and given direct suggestions that are not first filtered by the conscious mind. More important than anything, what Mesmer and Erickson brought to hypnotherapy is the idea that hypnosis can be used to heal.

The Healing Aspects of Revisiting Past Lives

A dancer in her twenties, Edith suffered from lupus erythematosus, a disease that was slowly making life as a dancer impossible. Her joints were stiffening and movement was becoming painful. She went to psychotherapist Dr. Roger Woolger, a graduate of Oxford who combines Western psychology with Eastern mysticism. During a hypnotic regression, Edith remembered a past life as a young Russian man involved in the anarchist movement. She recounted how the poor were rising up against their oppressors, who had been denying them food. In the uprisings the young man's father was killed by palace guards. The young man attempted to avenge his father by making a bomb, but instead the bomb went off, injuring his arms and legs.

Woolger took Edith through this past life experience

until she drew the correlation between the past life and her physical problems. Her disease went into remission once she made the correlation. Within six months she was pursuing her life's passion, which was dancing.

Therapists such as Woolger blend Western Jungian theory with Eastern Buddhist theories. From this approach, Woolger's philosophy of past lives is "Understanding what is really going on in past life therapy may not be that important—it's the results that count." In this sense, the question of whether the stories are true and can be confirmed ceases to be the crucial component. What is important is that remembering these past life experiences has a healing effect on the person doing the remembering.

Woolger explains, "You don't have to believe in reincarnation. Just accept that the unconscious mind will always come up with a story when healing is required." The main thing is to release energies that lock themselves into your physical body. By releasing these energies, you free a blockage, which allows you to heal. As Woolger says,

> From nearly a decade of taking clients and colleagues through past life experiences and continuing my own personal explorations, I have come to regard this technique as one of the most concentrated and powerful tools available to psychotherapy short of psychedelic drugs.

Like Woolger, Dr. Helen Wambach is a psychologist. Her quest into past lives began when she had a deja vu experience. Using hypnotherapy, she then began regressing groups of twelve or more people into past life experiences. She also began to accumulate data, leading her to say that past life recall while under hypnosis reflects the past, and that these recollections are much more than wishful fantasies created by the unconscious mind as proposed by traditional psychology experts.

The most profound aspect of Wambach's research is that many of the people, after recalling past life experiences, were cured of phobias and physical diseases, without any suggestion on the part of the hypnotherapist. All they did was go through the past life experience and nothing more. This revealed the remarkable fact that by remembering past lives, a person can sometimes heal her- or himself. This healing can occur even if that person didn't think it was possible.

The Spiritual Aspects of Past Lives

In 1933, the thirteenth Dalai Lama died. The senior lamas began a search for the next incarnation of the Dalai Lama. In Tibet, past lives are a common part of the people's spirituality, especially in terms of their spiritual leaders. In 1351, the first Dalai Lama was chosen because of his extraordinary wisdom, and since then every other Dalai Lama has been an incarnation of the first, retaining and adding to the knowledge through each lifetime. In this sense Dalai Lamas are not chosen; instead the task is more one of the senior lamas finding the right physical body that contains the soul of their spiritual leader.

In 1935, Tibet's regent, who was a senior lama, received a waking vision, and then a dream that led the search to the Kumbun Monastery in Amdo. Upon questioning, they heard tales of a little boy with extraordinary abilities in the neighboring village of Takster. The images of Amdo and Takster matched the regent's vision and dream.

Deciding to investigate the tales, the senior lamas sent Kewtsang Rinpoche, a high lama of Sera Monastery, along with a government official, to the village of Takster. To avoid detection, they dressed and acted like merchants on a business trip. They went to the house where the little boy lived and asked if they might be invited in for tea, a custom in Tibet. Once inside, Rinpoche was approached by a two-year-old boy named Lhamo Dhondrub, who sat on the man's lap and begin playing with the black rosary beads around the high lama's neck. These beads had been the possession of the thirteenth Dalai Lama. After playing with them for a while, the young boy declared that the beads belonged to him. With this assertion, Rinpoche then asked the boy if he knew the true identities of the two guests, to which Lhamo replied, "You are a lama of Sera." He also addressed the other man not only by his correct name, but also in the proper dialect of central Tibet, a dialect unknown in the boy's district.

Shortly thereafter, the men returned to test the boy's ability at remembering his past life as the thirteenth Dalai Lama, thus proving his incarnation as the fourteenth Dalai

Lama. For the test, the senior lamas had duplicates made of certain items owned by the previous lama. When shown both sets of the black and yellow rosaries, Lhemo without hesitation chose the ones owned by the Dalai Lama. In the other two tests, he chose the correct walking stick and eating bowl, even though the fake bowl was decorated much more intricately.

Lastly, the senior lamas examined the child for body marks distinctive to a Dalai Lama. These marks consist of large ears, long eyes, eyebrows curving up at the ends, streaks on the legs, and a mark in the shape of a conch shell on the palm of one hand. After examining the boy for these birthmarks, the senior lamas happily proclaimed that without a doubt they had found the fourteenth Dalai Lama.

Past lives connect us to the divine because that is ultimately where all creation originates, and within each lifetime there is birth, life, and death. These three concepts are constantly addressed within different spiritual traditions as in the Tibetan example. As we pass from life to life, we return to that in-between-ness, a cosmic soup that connects all there is into oneness, a point where we all come together, no matter what our race, creed, or spiritual orientation.

In Eastern traditions, past lives are stepping-stones, where, it is hoped, the soul moves forward, depending upon its actions and inactions. Much like Shakespeare's Hamlet, we are given choices that we can either act upon or not. How we deal with our past lives and integrate them into our present life can be a gauge as to how successful or happy we now find ourselves.

Past lives connect our past with our future, the present being a period of transition. This transition is toward a divine way of being that affects every minute aspect of our eternal spirit. This spirit is continually being reborn, and past lives are an expression of that rebirth and spiritual evolution, particularly in the case of the Dalai Lama. We are all Dalai Lamas in our own right. We only need to connect the dots and find out our purpose in this and every lifetime. Discovering our past lives is a way of doing just that.

Discovering Our Past Lives

Carol Bowman, author of *Children's Past Lives*, almost died in 1986 of pleurisy, asthma, pneumonia, and bronchial infections. Lying in her bed waiting to die, she spontaneously remembered a past lifetime in which she was a male musician dying of bronchial problems. As she went through the past life experience, she realized that the man was her. By moving through her death as this man, who died at the same age she was, Bowman realized she was replaying the past life. With that realization, she began to get better. She had been sick every winter of her present lifetime, but after the past life experience, she didn't get sick every winter. Not only did she get better and live, but she was healed from an affliction that seemed to come from another lifetime.

Maybe who we are is a result of all our past life experiences and personalities. Think about the possibility that we bring with us when we are born all of these experiences, but that most of us are just unaware of it. Each child is much more than a blank slate, waiting to be written upon by experience as science has led us to believe for so long. Anyone who has been around newborn babies knows they have personalities from the moment they are born, and maybe sooner.

Each of us is an accumulation of energies and experiences that are passed from lifetime to lifetime. We can choose to be aware of these connections, because ignorance does not diminish their effect. Moving beyond the veil of ordinary reality by using proven methods such as hypnosis and creative visualization, we can discover aspects of ourselves that can better help us understand who we are.

Each person is more than one individual and more than one incarnation. It may very well be that your personality, identifying you as a unique entity, remains essentially the same in all of your incarnations. Who you are as a whole is a combination of the experiences from many lifetimes. These experiences are the meaning behind the metaphysical concept that each person is a multitude or constellation of individuals.

All aspects of reality exist—all times, spaces, and forms, both visible and invisible. Simultaneously and within the context of multiple incarnations, each life you experience deepens your connection with oneness. Every lifetime happens simultaneously, and seems to occur at different times only because of your vantage point.

Life events appear to have a time definition to them because you are here in this physical earthly reality. Your body and attention are here, not somewhere else in time. Many well-documented cases of people such as Bridey Murphy do exist—people who have been able to recall dates, places, and names from what they know to be their past lives. Obviously the information is being tapped into by some faculty we inherently possess, albeit don't fully understand.

There are thousands of recorded cases of children recalling other time periods from the viewpoint of someone who died prior to the child's birth. The child usually voices thoughts and memories of this other person's personality and experiences. Bowman suggests four signs of past life memory: (1) matter-of-fact tone, (2) consistency over time, (3) knowledge beyond experience, and (4) corresponding behavior and traits. Not all past lives show all of the signs, but most often the signs appear in combination.

In past life regression, people often experience a lifetime as the opposite sex or with a dramatically different psychological makeup. Sometimes past life scenes are especially vivid, and may include not only images, but sounds, smells, impressions, sensory feelings, and strong emotions.

Past life regression can be used to call attention to patterns in your present life, helping you better understand both your positive and negative habits and characteristics. For example, you might find yourself repeating behaviors that are self-sabotaging or damaging to yourself and others. These often have a past life link that, once discovered, can be severed. By doing so you will find that the habit or behavior disappears.

Each time you do past life regression, either with others or alone, the experience can be enlightening and helpful, especially in regards to illness and relationships with people. After past life regression people often say, "Oh, that's the reason I have always felt that way about so-and-so."

By understanding past lifetimes, it is much easier to keep the different aspects of your life in perspective. The insights gained in past life regression transform you, helping you make the present life adjustments you desire, expanding your awareness, and leading you closer to personal enlightenment.

The Benefits
of Past Life Experiences

When you tap into past life experiences, it opens up the possibility that what you are tapping into is like a divine, uncorrupted Internet, an energy that is the accumulation of all energies. This macro-energy is often metaphysically referred to as oneness.

The question becomes, Are we accessing our personal past lives or an energetic membrane that encompasses all? No matter which is true, the healing and spiritual benefits of past life experiences are without question. They heal in ways that are unexplainable by traditional methods. Because they heal, the effects can't be negated even though traditional methods say it's not possible. As long as the experience enriches your immediate condition, knowing its origin is not essential. The benefits occur by working through the past life experience.

It's becoming harder and harder to ignore the facts presented before us. As more people learn about, and benefit from, knowing about and working with past life experiences, the possibilities are exciting, particularly because of their healing and spiritual potential.

By using the following past life regression, you can begin accessing your lifetimes and ridding yourself of any damaging internal baggage that you are carrying around from lifetime to lifetime. You can do this creative visualization as many times as you like, one lifetime per session. As you experience each lifetime, you need to process its experiences. By doing so, it will no longer deter you in your present life.

Past Life
Regression Visualization

The purpose of this visualization is to move your awareness backward in time and space to a past life. I suggest that you record the visualization in your own voice. Be sure you are not interrupted while recording the visualization. If you like, you can play soft music while you do the recording.

You can also ask someone such as your partner or a friend to read the visualization to you. Or you can read it yourself, a few lines at a time, and then close your eyes and imagine the scene playing out like a movie behind your eyelids. Then open your eyes, read a few more lines, and close your eyes and visualize. (See pages 4 and 5 for tips on reading the meditations.) It is always easier to visualize and move your mind backward in time when your eyes are closed because this facilitates the alpha state associated with meditation.

Start by getting as comfortable as you can. Unplug the phone or turn on your answering machine, and put the cell phone and pets out of the room so you won't be distracted.

Meditation

BEGIN BREATHING VERY GENTLY AND DEEPLY. SLOWLY CLOSE YOUR EYES. BREATHE IN SLOWLY TO THE COUNT OF THREE, STILL YOUR BREATH FOR THREE COUNTS, AND THEN EXHALE FOR THREE COUNTS. AS YOU DO THIS, FEEL YOURSELF BREATHING IN ENERGY AND BREATHING OUT ALL OF THE TENSIONS AND WORRIES OF THE DAY. DO THIS AT LEAST THREE TIMES.

CONTINUE TO BREATHE IN AND OUT SLOWLY AND RHYTHMICALLY, AND SLOWLY BEGIN TO IMAGINE YOURSELF GOING BACK IN TIME WITH EACH BREATH. AS YOU TAKE A DEEP BREATH IN, SEE YOURSELF ABOUT A YEAR AGO. WHAT ARE YOU DOING? WHERE ARE YOU LIVING? WHO ARE THE PEOPLE AROUND YOU?

WITH THE NEXT BREATH, IMAGINE YOURSELF FIVE YEARS AGO. AGAIN, NOTICE WHAT YOU ARE DOING,

THE HOUSE OR BUILDING WHERE YOU ARE LIVING, AND THE PEOPLE AROUND YOU.

AND THEN TAKE ANOTHER DEEP BREATH, AND IMAGINE YOURSELF TEN YEARS AGO. AGAIN, NOTICE WHAT YOU ARE DOING, WHERE YOU ARE LIVING, AND SOME OF THE PEOPLE AROUND YOU.

AS YOU KEEP BREATHING, SLOWLY AND COMPLETELY, BEGIN TO SEE YOURSELF AS A CHILD PLAYING AND LAUGHING, REMEMBERING THE HOUSE THAT YOU LIVED IN WHEN YOU WERE YOUNG. IMAGINE THE FACES OF SOME OF THE PEOPLE YOU LIKED WHEN YOU WERE A CHILD, SUCH AS PARENTS, GRANDPARENTS, SISTERS, BROTHERS, NEIGHBORS, OR FRIENDS.

TAKE ANOTHER DEEP BREATH AND MOVE BACK IN TIME. BECOME AN INFANT AND DISCOVER THE WORLD OF COLOR, LIGHT, SMELL, TOUCH, AND SOUND. MARVEL AT THE TREASURES AROUND YOU.

AS YOU BREATHE DEEPLY ONCE AGAIN, BEGIN TO REMEMBER BEING IN YOUR MOTHER'S WOMB, FEELING WARM, SECURE, AND SAFE.

TAKE ANOTHER DEEP AND COMPLETE BREATH AND, IN YOUR MIND'S EYE, IMAGINE MOVING INTO FREE FLOW, INTO ETHERIC SPACE, BREATHING AND FEELING THE ENERGY OF YOUR TRUE ESSENCE. IMAGINE YOURSELF AS PURE LIGHT, AS A BALL OF BRIGHT ENERGY.

IN YOUR MIND'S EYE, BEGIN TO SEE THE IMAGES OF WHAT SEEM TO BE TINY BUBBLES, EACH ONE

FILLED WITH A GOLDEN KEY. THESE BUBBLES FLOAT
BEHIND, BESIDE, IN FRONT, AND ALL AROUND YOU.
AS YOU FLOW FREELY, RELAXED AND CALM, YOU
REALIZE THAT THE KEYS ARE ENERGETIC KEYS THAT
CAN BE USED TO UNLOCK YOUR PAST LIFETIMES.

YOU ALLOW YOUR ESSENCE, THE PART OF YOU
THAT IS ETERNAL, TO SELECT THE KEY THAT UNLOCKS
THE DOOR TO ONE OF YOUR PAST LIVES, THE ONE
THAT YOU HAVE MOST TO LEARN FROM RIGHT NOW.

NOW FOCUS YOUR ATTENTION ON THE KEY-
FILLED BUBBLE THAT SEEMS THE MOST LIT UP, THE
BRIGHTEST, AND ENTER THE BUBBLE WITH YOUR
AWARENESS AND TAKE THE KEY. USE IT TO UNLOCK
A DOOR TO THE PAST, STEPPING THROUGH THE
THRESHOLD AND INTO A PAST LIFE.

AS YOU DO THIS, IMAGINE BEING IN THE PAST
LIFETIME YOU HAVE ENTERED. CHOOSE TO GO BACK
IN TIME, TO ANOTHER LIFETIME. BE THERE. TAKE A
DEEP BREATH, AND MOVE YOUR AWARENESS THERE.
THEN IN YOUR MIND'S EYE, LOOK DOWN AT YOUR
FEET. WHAT DO THEY LOOK LIKE IN THIS PAST LIFE-
TIME? ARE YOU WEARING SHOES OR ARE YOU BARE-
FOOT? IF YOU ARE BAREFOOT, WHAT DO YOUR FEET
LOOK LIKE? IF YOU ARE WEARING SHOES, WHAT ARE
THEY MADE OF? LEATHER, CLOTH, WOOD, OR SOME
OTHER MATERIAL? VERY SLOWLY, BEGIN TO CARE-
FULLY MOVE YOUR ATTENTION UP YOUR LEGS, SEEING
YOUR ANKLES AND KNEES. THEN LOOK AT YOUR
LEGS, THIGHS, PELVIS, STOMACH, CHEST, SHOULDERS,

ARMS, AND HANDS. MOVE YOUR HANDS OVER YOUR FACE AND FEEL ANY FACIAL HAIR THAT MIGHT BE THERE.

ARE YOU A WOMAN OR MAN IN THIS PAST LIFETIME? PERHAPS A BOY OR YOUNG GIRL? APPROXIMATELY HOW OLD ARE YOU? WHAT COLOR IS YOUR SKIN?

NOW IMAGINE LOOKING AT YOURSELF IN A MIRROR FOR A MOMENT. WHAT COLOR AND SHAPE ARE YOUR EYES IN THIS BODY? WHAT COLOR IS YOUR HAIR? IS IT SHORT OR LONG, CURLY OR STRAIGHT, COARSE OR FINE? OR ARE YOU BALD? ARE YOU WEARING ANYTHING ON YOUR HEAD?

SLOWLY NOW IN YOUR MIND'S EYE, BEGIN TO FOCUS ON YOUR HANDS IN THIS PAST LIFETIME, STUDYING THEM COMPLETELY. ARE THEY LARGE, SMALL, THICK, OR THIN? AS YOU STUDY YOUR HANDS, LOOK AT THEM CAREFULLY AND NOTICE WHETHER THERE ARE ANY RINGS ON YOUR FINGERS. IF YOU ARE WEARING A RING, EXACTLY WHAT DOES IT LOOK LIKE? WHAT IS IT MADE OF? DO YOU RECALL WHO GAVE IT TO YOU? PAY CLOSE ATTENTION TO THE SMALL DETAILS ON YOUR HANDS AND WRISTS. ARE THERE ANY OTHER DISTINGUISHING MARKS ON THEM?

AS YOU BREATHE IN DEEPLY AND COMPLETELY, AND RELAX EVEN MORE INTO THIS PAST LIFETIME, BEGIN TO BECOME AWARE OF WHAT IT FEELS LIKE TO BE IN THIS BODY. AND AS YOU CONTINUE TO

BREATHE DEEPLY AND SOFTLY AND RHYTHMICALLY,
LOOK CLOSELY AT WHAT YOU ARE WEARING OR NOT
WEARING. WHAT ARE THE COLORS AND FABRICS OF
YOUR CLOTHING? ARE YOUR CLOTHES OVERLY WARM
OR COLD, TIGHT OR LOOSE? WHAT IS THE STYLE?
IMAGINE FEELING THE TEXTURE OF THE MATERIALS
OF YOUR CLOTHING.

VERY SLOWLY, IN YOUR MIND'S EYE, BEGIN MOV-
ING IN THIS OTHER BODY, OBSERVING YOUR ACTIONS
AND NOTICING WHAT YOU ARE DOING. DO YOU KNOW
WHERE YOU ARE? DOES ANYTHING LOOK FAMILIAR
TO YOU? BEGIN TO VIEW YOUR SURROUNDINGS
SLOWLY AND THOROUGHLY, LOOKING AT THE
SCENERY AND BUILDINGS. MAKE A NOTE OF THE
LAND AROUND YOU. PERHAPS YOU KNOW WHAT
COUNTRY OR AREA YOU ARE IN. DO YOU KNOW WHAT
YEAR IT IS? PERHAPS YOU EVEN KNOW YOUR NAME IN
THIS LIFETIME. WHAT IS IT?

AS YOU LOOK AROUND, START WALKING. YOU
MAY BECOME AWARE OF OTHER PEOPLE AND OTHER
SOUNDS AROUND YOU AS WELL AS THE ANIMALS AND
PLANTS. INTERACT WITH THIS WORLD AND IN THIS
LIFETIME. BEGIN TO TALK WITH PEOPLE NEARBY, OR
TO EXPLORE THE AREA IN ANY WAY YOU CHOOSE,
USING YOUR DEEP BREATHING TO MOVE THROUGH
TIME. WITH EACH BREATH, YOU MOVE THROUGH
ANOTHER DAY, WEEK, MONTH, AND YEAR OF THIS
PAST LIFETIME. TAKE YOUR TIME TO EXPERIENCE THE
ENTIRETY OF IT. USE YOUR BREATH TO CLARIFY THE

IMAGES YOU MAY EXPERIENCE, BREATHING DEEPLY AND RELAXING EVEN MORE. TAKING DEEP AND COMPLETE BREATHS, USE YOUR RHYTHMIC BREATHING TO MOVE YOU FORWARD VERY SLOWLY AND GENTLY, THROUGH ALL THE YEARS OF THIS LIFETIME. SEE THE PAST LIFETIME TO ITS ENDING PLACE.

ALLOW YOURSELF TO RELEASE ALL THE NEGATIVE FEELINGS, PAIN, BAD EXPERIENCES, AND TRAUMAS FROM THIS PAST LIFETIME. JUST LET THEM GO, ONE BY ONE, RELEASING ANY NEGATIVE MEMORIES WITH YOUR EXHALED BREATH. DO THIS FOR AS LONG AS IT TAKES TO RELEASE ALL NEGATIVE ENERGIES FROM THIS PAST LIFETIME. AS YOU EXHALE THE PAIN AND NEGATIVITY, IMAGINE IT FLOATING AWAY FROM YOU WITH YOUR EXHALING BREATH, AND THEN INTO THE UNIVERSE, WHERE IT IS RECYCLED INTO POSITIVE ENERGY. ERASE ALL THE NEGATIVITY, PAIN, AND UNHAPPINESS FROM THIS PAST LIFETIME. JUST LET IT GO, NOW AND FOREVERMORE.

NOW TAKE ANOTHER DEEP AND CLEANSING BREATH, AND IMAGINE ALL THE POSITIVE EXPERIENCES FROM THIS PAST LIFETIME. IMAGINE EVERY MOMENT OF JOY, WONDER, EVERY EXPERIENCE OF LOVE AND HAPPINESS. SEE AND SENSE THESE POSITIVE MEMORIES OF BRIGHT AND BEAUTIFUL TIMES, USING THIS POSITIVE FEELING, THIS JOYFUL POWER TO STRENGTHEN YOU AND YOUR ESSENCE. JUST IMAGINE ABSORBING ALL THE GOOD, THE LOVE, THE JOY, THE ECSTASY, AND THE BLISS FROM THIS PAST

LIFETIME. BREATHE IT IN, ALL OF IT. FEEL IT CHARG-
ING AND ENRICHING YOU WITH POSITIVE POWER. DO
THIS FOR A FEW MINUTES.

AFTER YOU ARE FINISHED BREATHING IN THE
HAPPY AND JOYFUL TIMES FROM THIS PAST LIFETIME,
TAKE ANOTHER DEEP AND COMPLETE BREATH, AND
GENTLY FLOAT OUT OF THIS PAST LIFE, MOVING ONCE
AGAIN INTO FREE FLOW AND ETHERIC SPACE.

ONCE AGAIN, YOU FIND YOURSELF SURROUNDED
BY THE KEY-FILLED BUBBLES. FLOATING PEACEFULLY,
YOU FEEL MORE RELAXED THAN EVER BEFORE,
LIGHTER, MORE FREE, BRIGHTER, STRONGER, AND
TOTALLY EMPOWERED FROM YOUR PAST LIFE
JOURNEY.

TAKE A FEW MOMENTS AND FLOAT FREELY WITH
THE KEY-FILLED BUBBLES. YOU NOW UNDERSTAND
THAT THEY REPRESENT THE MANY LIFETIMES YOU CAN
EXPERIENCE. YOU REALIZE THAT YOU CAN RETURN
TO THIS PLACE WHENEVER YOU WANT TO DISCOVER
MORE OF YOUR PAST LIFETIMES.

SMILE TO YOURSELF AS YOU CONTINUE TO
BREATHE SOFTLY AND QUIETLY FOR A FEW MOMENTS.
THEN VERY SLOWLY BEGIN TO DIRECT YOUR ATTEN-
TION AND AWARENESS BACK TO YOUR PHYSICAL
BODY. SLIDE YOUR AWARENESS BACK INTO YOUR
PHYSICAL BODY LIKE YOU SLIDE A RING ONTO YOUR
FINGER, AND ENTER THE PRESENT MOMENT. NOTICE
THE LIGHT, AND ANY SOUNDS, SMELLS, AND OTHER
SENSATIONS AROUND YOU. REMEMBER YOUR ENTIRE

PAST LIFE EXPERIENCE AS YOU BREATHE YOURSELF
BACK TO THE ROOM COMPLETELY, MOVING YOUR
HANDS AND FEET. NOW OPEN YOUR EYES WITHOUT
REALLY FOCUSING THEM ON ANYTHING.

TAKE ANOTHER DEEP BREATH, STRETCH YOUR
BODY, AND COME BACK TO THE PRESENT MOMENT,
FOCUSING YOUR EYES IN FRONT OF YOU. COMPLETE
THE VISUALIZATION BY CLAPPING YOUR HANDS THREE
TIMES.

☞ *When you are finished, be sure to jot down any
notes from your past life experience.*

CHAPTER THREE

Karma,
The Great
Balancer

As people think so they are, both here and hereafter, thoughts being things, the parent of all actions, good and bad alike, and as the sowing has been, so will the harvest be.

The Tibetan Book of the Dead

The Many Faces
of Karma

In her book *Reliving Past Lives*, Dr. Helen Wambach recounts the past lives of Betty, whom she describes as "a pleasant middle-aged woman with remarkable psychic abilities." Wambach regressed Betty to five different lives between the years 1400 and 1900. During one particular lifetime in the mid-1800s, Betty reported a life as James Buchanan, fifteenth president of the United States, just before Abraham Lincoln and the Civil War.

Speaking as Buchanan, she said, "The purpose of my life was to demonstrate that single-minded devotion to work and high ambition could result in high achievement." This proved to be true on a professional level because he became president of the United States, but unfortunately his personal life was empty. In Betty's words, "As Buchanan I was lonely and had little affection in this life." The idea that actions and outcome are proportionately linked to each other is the basis for karma.

Karma has many faces, one of which was expressed by the philosophical and spiritual thinkers of classical Greece, who came to the conclusion that humans have a divine self, but at the same time a much larger "negative" self that derives from the Titans, a race of giants who were the original race of gods and goddesses in not only Greek mythology, but also Celtic, Roman, and Norse mythology.

In the Greek concept of reincarnation, the more

people come back on the earthly plane, the greater their chance of making their divine self a greater part of themselves than their negative self. In particular, the Greeks expressed the idea that people would be rewarded or punished in the next human or animal incarnation, depending on how they lived their present life.

Karma means "cause." By contrast, "vipaka" means "effect," which is what karma works toward. As a human being, your karma comes through your thoughts and actions and how you conduct yourself through life. Because karma is tied to the "cause" of life, it is essentially the purpose for being. Simply put, your purpose or karma in life is to achieve your effect, something that is different for each person, but is ultimately the same for all people—to once again become one spirit with the divine.

In terms of reincarnation, two ideas make up the basics of karma. The first idea proposes that there is a balancing force in the universe. The second idea is that all things move in a forward motion, and are continually evolving on a physical, mental, and spiritual level. Working together these two forces play an important part in understanding possibly how reincarnation happens and why it works as a tool for personal health and spiritual understanding.

The concept that things balance out both in this lifetime and other lifetimes is a universal theme among spiritual traditions throughout the world. The Golden Rule as given in Matt. 7:12 says, "Whatsoever ye would that men should so do to you, do ye also unto them." In other words, treat others the way you want to be treated by others. Move toward what you want.

In contrast, the Silver Rule says, "Do not unto others whatsoever you would not have them do unto you," which is the same concept in the negative. In other words, don't do anything to anyone else that you don't want done to you. Move away from what you don't want.

The underlying idea is that doing to another as another does to you has the effect of balancing the polarities of life. If you do something positive to a person, that individual will do something positive for you. If you do something negative to a person, that individual will do something negative to you. This is the practical application of both the Golden and Silver rules. This balancing concept is expressed in many major religions, suggesting that it may be a basic component to spirituality as a whole.

Many spiritual traditions talk about the idea in terms of the balance between light and dark, good and evil. In Hindu mythology, Devi is the goddess whose balancing forces stop the world from falling into chaos. What this points to is that each deed and action spawns other deeds and actions that are affected and balanced by the original act. Moving through time and space, these take on proportions that are eventually infinite in their scope.

In terms of people it means that every person you come into contact with is influenced in some way by the interaction with you. It is a forever connection. It's like an energetic imprint. Your energy field interacts with the other person's energy field. This person then goes out and interacts with ten or twenty other people, who then interact with another ten or twenty, and the numbers rise quickly.

You can demonstrate how your actions affect the actions of others with a group of people at a meeting or in an office. Start by going over to someone and being really positive and uplifting in what you say to them. If you can, sit back and watch how this feeling spreads.

Usually what happens is that that person is suddenly having a better day because she or he just had a positive experience, and she or he then transfers this energy to the next person, who also suddenly has a positive experience. This may seem simplistic, but it is the way things work. Basically, when you spread positive feelings and actions out into the world, these actions start a positiveness that is then taken and spread a thousandfold, depending on how many people you come into contact with in a day.

Unfortunately, this technique also works in the reverse, meaning that if you spend too much time in the negative darkness, it will consume you. This is a bet I would take to Las Vegas. The idea, when it comes to the balancer, is to keep your thoughts and actions in a place that is consistent with your personal patterns. Otherwise you will find yourself in a struggle, both in terms of ego and self.

Once again the idea is balance rather than struggle. Life is often a matter of balancing forces that seem poles apart, as Rudyard Kipling wrote in the poem "If"—"If you can keep your head about you when all about you are losing theirs." That is obviously one of the keys to existence, no matter what your perception of reality. Like the tides of the ocean, the spiritual forces of humanity recede and rise according to the feelings and expressions of the populace.

Balance is only one part of karma; the other part involves the evolution of the soul. Many cultures say either that souls move from the mortal to the divine or that they are already divine and seek to get back to their original condition. The soul's evolution is expressed by many cultures in a number of ways. In a scientific sense, the spiritual evolves just like the physical and cultural.

An example of the divine to mortal, and mortal to divine concept is the Tuatha De Danann in Celtic mythology. Not only is each god and goddess descended from the mother goddess, Danu, but each Celt also stems from her. There is a definite kinship between mortals and deities. Accordingly, many of the Tuatha De Danann were originally mortals who only later, through time, became the mythological goddesses and gods.

This suggests that there is a spiritual evolution occurring that mirrors our physical evolution. Reincarnation, by virtue of this mirroring aspect, infers that we are living multiple lives; our purpose therefore is to evolve as human beings.

The varied philosophic and spiritual traditions around the world talk about this transition and evolvement, usually to divineness, in ways that involve lifetimes. This gives a very basic reason for reincarnation: we are progressing and evolving spiritually much like we are physically and mentally. It makes perfect sense that the three faces of body, mind, and spirit would evolve both individually and as a whole. This continual evolving is what reincarnation, and as a result, karma, is all about. We are all progressing to godhood and goddesshood. It is part of our programming that may actually be encoded in our DNA. Recent scientific studies suggest that there is a specific part of our brain, called the God center, that connects us to the divine.

The Fusion of Karma and Reincarnation

Also included in Wambach's *Reliving Past Lives* is the case of Shirley, who lived a past life in which she was a sensitive, or psychic. In that lifetime, she tried to heal a boy who was dying. When the boy died, the people in the town chased her off a cliff. When she awakened from the session in which she had revisited the experience, she felt dizzy and had an immediate need to run. But since regressing to the lifetime in which she was a sensitive, Shirley in her current lifetime has ceased to have what she used to call "dizzy spells."

What karma does for reincarnation is give a reason for being. We reincarnate into different beings because we are seeking to balance both our positive and negative elements into one being that propels us into divineness. Our humanness and ego tie us to this reality, and our spirit and divineness compel us to move forward and attain oneness.

In the Buddhist teachings, the law of karma in its

basic form says that for every event that occurs, there will follow another event whose existence was caused by the first. This second event will be pleasant or unpleasant depending on whether its cause was primarily positive or negative.

In the words of Gautama Buddha,

For, owners of their deeds (karma) are the beings, heirs of their deeds; their deeds are the womb from which they sprang; with their deeds they are bound up; their deeds are their refuge. Whatever deeds they do—good or evil—of such they will be the heirs. And wherever the beings spring into existence, there their deeds will ripen; and wherever their deeds ripen, there they will earn the fruits of those deeds, be it in this life, or be it in the next life, or be it in any other future life.

From the standpoint of Confucianism, everyday situations are an opportunity to treat others as you wish they would treat you. Living with "Jen" (the soul of all virtues), you find inner fulfillment. Other people's actions need not force you to wander from your path. Instead, the interaction with others offers you an opportunity to reach out with human understanding. Deep within each human being is a positive human nature lying dormant, waiting to be awakened, to be enlightened. After all, there are many paths to follow, but they all lead to oneness, where all spiritualities converge into one divine path.

Some African tribes believe that the soul, which they

call "orka," is divine in origin. It exists before birth and after death. After death, they reunite with their dead ancestors. One of the beliefs is that the dead reincarnate into their same ancestral families, at least their dominant qualities do. In a sense, it is like a form of energetic cloning, where the patterns and tendencies are reincarnated, not the personality characteristics that make up the human ego.

When someone reincarnates they become a new soul, but also continue to live in the afterlife. Some tribes believe that if souls do not fulfill their destiny in one life, they come back until they do. Those who have good characters and live a good life will journey into a new life filled with divineness, which is truly "home." Those who don't measure up in a lifetime are destined to live in a hot, dry environment where people eat centipedes and earthworms.

The Albert Brooks film *Defending Your Life* brilliantly expresses the vast differences in lifetimes. One of the main characters who is a compassionate person was Joan of Arc in a past lifetime, whereas the other main character, who is sort of a business shark, was, as he put it, "lunch." (He was chased through the jungle, and caught, by a large carnivore.)

All of this again points to the idea that your thoughts, actions, and deeds in life as they pertain to your overall pattern are what carry over lifetime after lifetime. In modern physics, these are called tendencies. They are the basic foundation of everything.

From a particle to a wave, everything has a tendency, certain proclivities or patterns that make it unique from everything else. Like a fingerprint, your pattern differentiates you from anyone and anything else. Like a wave, patterns are replicated through time, both genetically and energetically.

Swami Sivananda says, "Every action that you do produces a two-fold effect. It produces an impression in your mind and when you die you carry the Samskara in the Karmashaya or receptacle of works in your subconscious mind. It produces an impression on the world or Akashic records."

Each action is imprinted in a sort of energetic code that is seemingly eternal. Although both Western and Eastern traditions have karmic values to their teachings, they differ in their perceptions of karma. Western cultures see it more as an immediate value that is balancing, whereas Eastern cultures see it as much more extended, evolving through lifetimes. Beyond this, both cultures have similarities with respect to the basic ideas of karma that give it a universal quality, that moves beyond the boundaries of culture, time, or locale. This is also why karma is important in the understanding of reincarnation, in the sense that it gives it purpose.

The Eastern View of Karma

The Svetasvtara Upanishad says,

The individual self, augmented by its aspirations, sense contact, visual impressions and delusion, assumes successive forms in accordance with its actions; So it is that we live in accordance with our deep, driving desire. It is this desire at the time of death that determines what our next life is to be. We will come back to Earth to work out the satisfaction of that desire.

The term "karma" seems to have originated with the Hindu Upanishads of the sixth century BCE. In the Eastern view of karma, a person's essence or energy is continually reborn into physical form until they reach a divine state of being. In a specific lifetime, karma is assessed in terms of a person's life mission. In terms of multiple lifetimes, it becomes an evolutionary process that each life's mission works toward; otherwise the person must come back and learn the lesson in another physical form.

Realizing and fulfilling your life's mission or calling is an important part of the Eastern view of karma. As you fulfill each lifetime's mission, you progress toward your eventual spiritual goal: being one with the divine. When you achieve this oneness, you no longer need to return to physical form. You remain in that energetic and spiritual place of divinity. The Hindus call this divine state of being moksha and the Buddhists refer to it as nirvana.

The main difference between the Hindu and Buddhist point of view is that Hindus believe in the rebirth of the soul, whereas the Buddhists believe in the rebirth of the spirit, but not the soul. I would like to briefly explore these similarities and differences.

Hinduism is a religion and spiritual philosophy that welcomes individual interpretation of its doctrines and ideas. In its basic form, the soul travels through transmigration, meaning that a soul travels from body to body. In Hinduism, the soul or "god within" is called the atman. After many times of being reborn or reincarnated, the atman achieves moksha. At that point, it is no longer reincarnated into physical form. Like life, reincarnation follows a sequence, from the physical to the spiritual.

Within the context of Hindu Brahmanism, people's actions in a former life determine how they act in their present life. All previous bad deeds need to be atoned for, and positive patterns are continued because the eventual purpose is to evolve toward divinity. People are forgiven for misdeeds because they are working out their karma in this life from past lives and creating karma in this life to be worked out in future lifetimes. In this way, karma has both temporal and nontemporal aspects.

As a comparison, the notion of an individual progressing through numerous lifetimes is a key part of the teachings of Buddha. During his enlightenment experience, Buddha clearly saw all the previous existences he'd gone through, revealing among other things "the transcendent greatness of the Dharma in comparison to the brief, fragmentary nature of a single life span." Buddha went on to say that no separate factor such as soul, self, or personal imprint gets passed along. It is more a process of rebirth rather than reincarnation. "The quality of one life determines the quality of the next one in a causal way, much like the transference of the flame of one candle to another." The link between one life and another is a "karmic energy surge." The karmic aspect relates to the condition of the being (will, wisdom, heart) that is dying. The cause of the impulse of surge is the final instant of the life as well as its overall mental history. Buddha said that rebirth arises from two causes. The last thought of the previous life is its governing principle, and the actions of the previous life are its basis. The last thought is known as decease, the appearance of the first thought as rebirth.

The Dalai Lama is the current incarnation of the original Buddha. As such, he is born with karmic memory of his previous lives. In this context the knowledge and teachings of Buddha are passed down and essentially reborn with each generation. Within this spiritual context, the purpose of the Dalai Lama and the Buddha energy that he carries forth is to help other people in their quest for nirvana, both as a teacher and one who exemplifies what he teaches.

Hinduism and Buddhism both believe in reincarnation and karma, but disagree in their view of how this process is accomplished. In the Hindu motif, the soul, or atman, is reincarnated or transmigrated into many forms before finally reaching moksha, and is no longer reincarnated into physical form.

In the Buddhist motif, the "anatta," meaning "without a soul," moves from one life to another, working out its karma until reaching nirvana, where it is no longer reincarnated in physical form. In this motif, it is the person's patterns and basic essence that are reincarnated rather than the actual self, more akin in some ways to a person's spirit. This again brings up the question of what is soul and what is spirit. Frankly, at times, it seems mostly a matter of semantics and perception.

The Western View of Karma

Scientific, literary, and philosophical scholar Rudolph Steiner said,

> *Just as an age was ready to receive the Copernican theory of the universe, so is our own age ready for the ideas of reincarnation and karma to be brought into the general consciousness of humanity. And what is destined to happen in the course of evolution will happen no matter what powers rise up against it.*

Although essentially an Eastern concept, karma has been readily accepted by the Western world. Mainly because of its universal aspects, the ideas of karma prevail throughout Western mythology and culture. But unlike Eastern thought, which sees karma more as a cause moving toward an effect, Western thought views karma more in terms of both cause and effect. Drawing it all the way out, people in the West tend to view karma as a force that balances "good" actions and "bad" actions. The "good" live the virtuous life, whereas the "bad" get what is coming to them, which in the Christian Western tradition is called hell.

Christian mythology includes several concepts and accounts that are built around the balancing aspect of karma. It starts with the "original sin," where Adam and Eve are punished in a karmic sense for Eve's supposed misdeeds, and ends with Judgment Day, when every person is evaluated according to their deeds on Earth and it is determined whether they go to heaven, purgatory, or hell. In between, Jesus Christ is born, martyred, and resurrected, eventually becoming a symbol much like Buddha, one of teaching people how to reach communion with the divine.

Retributive justice—for example, an eye for an eye—is a form of karma that says that if you do someone harm in this life, they will do you harm in a future lifetime. This eye for an eye view is very straightforward, A to B, and as such, is a key concept in the criminal justice systems of the Western world.

The concept of compensation is an evolved form of retributive justice that is not as direct in its approach. This form of karma says that if you do harm to someone in this life, that person may not necessarily harm you in the same way in a future life, but you will have to compensate that individual in some way for the harm done.

Both of these Western views of karma show it as a force that balances people's actions and the energies that come from them. This idea permeates much of Western culture to the point where many people see themselves as instruments of karma, evidenced by the expression "I'm going to teach that person a lesson they'll never forget." Films and television shows often play out the instrument of karma theme. The hero is first mistreated by the villains, and then comes back to seek revenge and right the wrong.

How Karma Affects Reincarnation

In the words of Edwin Hubbel Chapin, a nineteenth-century author and theologian, "Every action of our lives touches on some chord that will vibrate in eternity." Every action, indeed every thought, creates a reaction or response in oneness. Just think a moment about the immense potential of your thoughts and actions in this context!

Karma provides a framework of a possible reason for past lives and reincarnation. In one respect, we are constantly being reborn and nothing truly dies. In a second respect, there is a force that both balances and evolves. Tie these two ideas together and suddenly you have something that begins to thread together ideas that give light to this abstract, and for the most part subjective, topic. One of the themes of this book is to put these subjective views together in a way so that everyone can understand their universal implications. There are such things as random events, but most events are usually a matter of perception and purpose.

Rather than being an external judge and jury that determines compensation through lifetimes, karma and reincarnation are forces generated by our tendencies and patterns. In a sense we have a personal and universal self. Our personal self becomes identified with our soul, whereas our universal self is discussed in terms of spirit.

We each have a personalized rule-maker and rule-keeper that psychologist Sigmund Freud called the parental superego. This superego has a definite influence on our overall pattern, connecting back to our overall karma. Our parental superego is generated from our socialization; no matter how far we progress, we are continually reminded as to where we originated.

On a more karmic and reincarnation level, the superego relates to those patterns that we transmit from lifetime to lifetime. The research done on past lives strongly suggests that there are people in our lives who show up in multiple lifetimes. Many spiritual traditions suggest that we have energetic or spiritual connections with certain people. They are our soul group. These connections are similar to the difference between particles and waves, the individual and the whole.

One thing each of us learns as we move through life is that the world is not necessarily a just or fair one. But as we continue to make choices, adapt to life changes, and move through different situations, things begin to even out. We are the result of the patterns that we put in place. What our experiences serve to do is to give us more awareness into how the oneness of the universe operates. If you toss a coin enough times the numbers of heads and tails pretty much equal out. Karma and past lives work much the same way. The balancing is done over multiple lifetimes.

Discovering Your Karma in Your Present Lifetime

The great Indian statesman Mahatma Gandhi had a dream one night that showed him the path of peaceful resistance that became his calling in life. The idea that people have a calling or mission in life is another universal concept. For instance, what if each lifetime were but a day in a larger lifetime? Let's say at the beginning of each day or lifetime, you sat down and wrote a list of things to do that day, that lifetime. The karmic element comes in at the end of the day or lifetime when you see how many of the things you accomplished.

In addition to Gandhi, many other historical figures, including Rene Descartes and Albert Einstein, have connected through dreams with what became their calling in life. This suggests a link between dreams and the forces that call to you, hoping you'll be aware enough to answer that call, and remember what you were supposed to do in this lifetime. In a sense this is the element that joins this lifetime together with past and future lifetimes.

The Chippewa Indians of the upper midwest United States believe that you can live out both past and future lives in your dreams. In this perception, it is understandable that dreams are a means of accessing your calling in this lifetime, which in a karmic sense is seen in terms of your past and future lives and your overall patterns and proclivities.

We each have a calling in life that is innate. We instinctually gravitate toward certain things, and by the same reasoning, follow particular paths rather than others. Many of us take Robert Frost's proverbial "Road Not Taken," and follow the path less traveled by, so that we can truly follow our heart and spirit. These patterns and tendencies happen simultaneously on many levels, including the physical, mental, and spiritual. The integration or balancing of these levels is what the study of karma is all about.

Carol Bowman in her intriguing book *Return from Heaven* documents the case of a two-year-old named Dylan, who began exhibiting odd behavior. He said that he smoked cigarettes and he used his cardboard pogs as dice while calling out, "Sevens, I'm throwing sevens." On his third birthday, he received a toy gun that soon became the obsession of his life. He took it everywhere, when he was swimming, eating, and even to bed. The behavior drove his parents crazy, but they didn't know what to do about it.

After conversations with Dylan's aunt and mother, Bowman learned that Dylan's behavior mirrored the patterns of his late grandfather, who as a policeman and prison guard, had habitually smoked and played dice, and never went anywhere without his gun. Also, when talking about it, Dylan's mother realized that she and Dylan's father had never said good-bye to the grandfather because they weren't there when he died, plus they missed the funeral. She felt this accounted for her young son's reluctance to say good-bye, which often made saying good night at bedtime very uncomfortable.

When you die with "unfinished business," it can often stay with you into the next lifetime, or other future lifetimes, waiting to be worked out in a karmic sense. When Dylan's parents acknowledged his past life memories as his grandfather, he quit obsessing about taking the toy gun everywhere. Also, the problem with good-byes began diminishing. Basically, this was a karmic experience that had a healing effect in Dylan's current lifetime, especially in terms of his family.

Your Life Mission and Dharma

The idea of "unfinished business" is common in past life regressions. Dr. Helen Wambach says, "This experience of sorrow at death because of duties unfulfilled occurs in regressions. The grief seems to be related to other people, rather than felt for the self." What this all points to is the concept that in each lifetime you have a mission that includes things you would like to accomplish in that lifetime. Eastern spiritual traditions have a concept called dharma that relates to this concept of a life's mission.

Hinduism contains a group of texts known as Dharmashastras or the teachings of dharma. "Dharma" is loosely translated as "religion," "law," or "righteousness," and deals with the first human aspiration or value, which is virtue, duty, and the practice of religion and spirituality in an individual sense. In addition, "moksha," which is the fourth human aspiration, is the divine knowledge that leads to self-realization and liberation from "the wheel of samsara" or "the wheel of rebirth."

As mandala-like visions of the structure of the universe, dharma in the Buddhist sense refers not only to the main body of Buddhist teachings, but also to the entire universe that is constantly teaching you when you are aware (awake) enough to learn. Additionally, "dharma kaya" speaks of the absolute truth or Buddha nature. Everyone has Buddha nature, an identity that is not separate, but instead is shared with all other beings as well as the absolute (divine). Enlightenment involves realizing this Buddha nature. In fact, joy and happiness stem from connecting, even if just for a moment, with your Buddha nature.

Universally, the concept of dharma relates to the agreements that you make for a particular lifetime. In karmic terms, following your dharma assures that you will be rewarded in the next lifetime because you subscribe to a higher order. This higher "divine" order determines the individual lifetime as well as the overall scheme of things as delineated over many lifetimes, and is seen as the evolution of the soul or spirit.

Karma, the Big Picture

Imagine that each day, you awaken and are reborn into a new lifetime, and then as nighttime falls, you die and enter a state of sleep until the next day, when you are again reborn into another lifetime. This pattern happens every day or every lifetime. In terms of the whole, it becomes part of "the greater lifetime" that includes and is made up of each day of the individual lifetimes. Each of us has a greater lifetime. This greater lifetime is the main theme behind both karma and reincarnation.

An excellent example of this movement toward greater lifetimes can be found in the Hawaiian belief system. In this system, you are incarnated in stages that progress from rock to water, to vegetable, to insect, to bird, to animal, and finally to human. There is no division between the element, flora, fauna, and mortals. Instead it is a natural progression into more complex beings.

In the Hindu belief system, souls progress through an ascending stratum of human want. This progression doesn't necessarily take the form of a straight line, but instead resembles a fumbling and zigzagness that eventually progresses toward individual goals. In the long term, the trend is upward. It involves a movement away from attachments to physical objects and sensual stimuli. It also involves a movement toward an evolvement of the spiritual self that eventually links you to the divine whole or oneness.

Part of karma is about understanding how this lifetime relates to the whole of all lifetimes. Each life's mission relates to the greater lifetime. By understanding and coming to grips with your greater lifetime, you see what you need to do in this lifetime. It's like looking at a road map. If you travel on this road, it leads to the next road, which in the end should lead you to the place where you want to be. This is what karma and oneness is all about—the coming together of many streams of energy into the whole. Rather than being a punishing judge and jury, karma is more a power that moves you forward in your rebirth and reincarnation process. It is a spiritual door to oneness.

Karma infers that you perceive your life within the context of the greater picture. It also infers a sense of self-responsibility that allows no loopholes. You are what you are, which is who you made yourself to be—in this lifetime, through past lives, and in your overall life experience. Karma is about seeing how your present and future affect this greater picture. In Eastern terms, this sight brings enlightenment, and karma is the lens to look through to get there.

Much like evolution, karma infers forward movement. You evolve much of the time through your personal relationships with other people and the divine. The idea is not to leave a lot of baggage behind that needs to be dealt with in future lifetimes. The old adage "Keep it simple" applies here. The less you stir up the karmic cauldron, the less baggage you have to carry in other lifetimes. Accordingly, the more positivity you put out this lifetime, the more positivity you will experience in your next lifetime.

Often, understanding your past and future brings your present into perspective. This is where the value of past life regression comes in. It has great therapeutic use because it offers useful information about your present lifetime, here and now.

Everything is connected together in a web of oneness that is akin to the Buddha nature. As you become aware of your karmic self, you begin to understand the patterns that make up who you are as a complete being. With this knowledge and understanding comes the ability to use karma as a tool for healing and spiritual growth. The following meditation is intended to help you in that process. It enlists the powers of your spiritual guide or helper to discover your life purpose. The meditation will help you better understand your karma, and show how body, mind, and spirit are one.

Meditation for Balancing Your Lifetimes

In the competitive, material world, many of us use all of our energy just struggling to survive. Our egos are trained to consume material things beyond our needs or wants. This accentuates our separateness. Being disconnected and unbalanced perpetuates the ever-present modern madness, and it also keeps us from our life purpose.

Karma and reincarnation are ways of breaking this veil of separateness. They reconnect you with the oneness of all things.

The following meditation can help you reconnect with that oneness by communicating with your spirit guide to better understand your life choices. Choice is critical to personal success in life. After all, success is the name we give to the desirable results we would like to attain through our thoughts and actions.

The Balancing Your Lifetimes Meditation is most powerful when tape-recorded in your own voice and played back as often as you like. The best times to listen to the meditation are just upon waking and just before going to sleep. These are the times when you will gain the most benefit from the process.

If you prefer, you can have a friend slowly read the meditation to you. Or you can read it to yourself, following along a paragraph at a time. (See pages 4 and 5 for tips on reading the meditation.)

Before doing the meditation, turn on your answering machine, turn off the ringer, or unplug your phone. Tell your family that you don't want to be disturbed for about thirty minutes. Put the dog, cat, and the cell phone out of the room to avoid interruptions while meditating.

Next, get comfortable. Sit or recline, uncrossing your ankles and arms. Loosen any clothing, belts, shoes, wrist-watches, or jewelry that might be binding you.

I also suggest that you anoint yourself with lavender oil. Dab oil on both wrists, ankles, and the back of your head. The fragrance of the oil stimulates psychic abilities and promotes altered states of consciousness that are helpful when communicating with your spirit guide.

Meditation

BEGIN THE MEDITATION BY TAKING A DEEP BREATH AND EXHALING IT COMPLETELY. AS YOU BREATHE IN, IMAGINE THAT YOU ARE BREATHING IN PURE ENERGY. AS YOU BREATHE OUT, IMAGINE RELEASING ALL OF YOUR TENSIONS AND WORRIES THROUGH YOUR EXHALED BREATH.

NEXT, BEGIN TO BREATHE RHYTHMICALLY. BREATHE IN TO THE COUNT OF THREE, HOLDING YOUR BREATH FOR THREE COUNTS AND THEN EXHALING COMPLETELY. DO THIS THREE TIMES OR MORE, DEEPLY BREATHING IN AND OUT, RELAXING MORE AND MORE. JUST ALLOW ALL OF THE TENSIONS, STRESSES, AND WORRIES OF THE DAY TO MOVE OUT OF YOUR BEING, MORE AND MORE WITH EACH EXHALED BREATH.

LET YOURSELF RELAX EVEN MORE, AND ALLOW YOUR MIND TO FLOAT FREE. ANY SOUNDS YOU MAY HEAR IN THE ROOM, SUCH AS THE TICKING OF A CLOCK OR THE SOUND OF YOUR DEEP BREATHING, JUST HELP YOU TO RELAX EVEN MORE. FEEL A SENSE OF PEACEFULNESS COMPLETELY SURROUNDING YOU.

NOW CLOSE YOUR EYES, AND BEGIN TO IMAGINE A STREAM OF FLOWING WHITE LIGHT IN YOUR MIND'S EYE. IMAGINE YOURSELF STANDING IN FRONT OF THE STREAM AND THEN WALKING OVER TO IT. FEEL THE PLEASING WARMTH OF THE WHITE LIGHT. NOW IMAGINE WALKING EFFORTLESSLY INTO THE STREAM, FEELING IT ALL AROUND YOU.

SLOWLY BREATHE THE FLOWING, BRIGHT, WHITE LIGHT INTO YOUR BODY. BREATHE IN THE STREAM OF WHITE LIGHT THROUGH EVERY PORE OF YOUR SKIN, INHALING AND EXHALING WHITE LIGHT. AS YOU BREATHE IN THE BRIGHT LIGHT, FEEL IT FLOWING THROUGH YOUR BODY, COURSING THROUGH YOU LIKE

A RIVER OF LIGHT, AND WARMING YOU FROM THE TOP
OF YOUR HEAD TO THE TIPS OF YOUR TOES.

FEEL THE WARM WHITE LIGHT COMPLETELY
FILLING YOU. IMAGINE IT BECOMING RADIANT,
EMPOWERING, AND HEALING AS IT WARMS EVERY
CELL OF YOUR ENTIRE BODY. FEEL THE LIGHT FLOW-
ING THROUGH YOU AND RELAXING YOU EVEN MORE.

AS YOU BECOME MORE RELAXED, FEELING
PEACEFUL AND CALM, YOUR MIND BECOMES QUIET,
YET YOU REMAIN ALERT AND AWARE. IN THIS STATE
OF MIND, YOU BEGIN TO SENSE SOMEONE THERE
WITH YOU IN THE PLEASING STREAM OF WHITE LIGHT.
AT FIRST YOU MAY FEEL THE UNDENIABLE SENSE
THAT SOMEONE IS RIGHT NEXT TO YOU. THEN, LIKE A
LIGHT WITHIN LIGHT, YOUR SPIRIT GUIDE APPEARS OUT
OF THE STREAM OF WHITE LIGHT.

WHEN YOUR GUIDE APPEARS, ASK FOR HER
OR HIS NAME. OFTEN THE NAME IS SIMPLE AND
UNASSUMING. ONCE YOU KNOW YOUR SPIRIT GUIDE'S
NAME, CALL HER OR HIM BY NAME WHENEVER YOU
INTERACT. SUDDENLY YOU REALIZE THAT YOU HAVE
KNOWN YOUR SPIRIT GUIDE FOR EONS OF TIME, AND
THAT YOU ALREADY KNOW HER OR HIS NAME IN THE
DEPTH OF YOUR SPIRIT.

YOUR SPIRIT GUIDE HAS THE COMFORTING
PRESENCE OF A DIVINE FRIEND. SHE OR HE IS YOUR
HELPER THROUGH LIFETIMES, AND IS HERE NOW TO
COMMUNICATE WITH AND HELP YOU. A POWERFUL
BEING OF LIGHT WITH A DEEP UNDERSTANDING OF

YOUR LIFETIMES AND YOUR MOTIVATIONS, WHETHER IN HUMANLIKE OR ANGELIC FORM, YOUR GUIDE WATCHES OVER YOU AND PROTECTS YOU FROM HARM.

YOUR GUIDE CAN HELP YOU DISCOVER YOUR PURPOSE, YOUR LIFE MISSION. SHE OR HE KNOWS OF YOUR MANY LIFETIMES AND HOW THEY ALL CONNECT INTO ONE. BY COMMUNICATING WITH YOUR SPIRIT GUIDE, YOU CAN BETTER UNDERSTAND THE CIRCUM- STANCES OF YOUR LIFE AND THE PEOPLE IN IT. YOU WILL HAVE A DEEPER UNDERSTANDING OF WHO YOU ARE THIS LIFETIME AND THE CHOICES YOU MAKE.

WITH THE HELP OF YOUR SPIRIT GUIDE YOU CAN SEE BEYOND THE PRESENT MOMENT, AND GLIMPSE INTO THE PAST AND FUTURE. REALIZE THAT EVERY- THING THAT IS YOU IS STILL HERE, INCLUDING ALL OF YOUR PERSONAL MEMORIES AND THE HISTORY OF YOUR MANY LIFETIMES.

YOUR SPIRIT GUIDE HELPS YOU WORK WITH YOUR ISSUES, BOTH IN THIS LIFETIME AND IN OTHERS. SHE OR HE CAN HELP YOU FIND THE ROOT OF ANY PROB- LEMS YOU MAY BE FACING.

AS YOU STAND TOGETHER IN THE STREAM OF FLOWING WHITE LIGHT, YOUR GUIDE SPEAKS:

"LISTEN TO YOUR HEART. FEEL WHAT CHOICES FEEL RIGHT AND WHICH DO NOT. WITH EVERY CHOICE YOU MAKE YOU CHART YOUR JOURNEY THIS LIFETIME, AND YOU BALANCE YOUR MANY LIFETIMES. WITNESS HOW YOUR CHOICES ARE MADE. EVALUATE THEIR OUTCOME. HOW DO YOUR CHOICES INFLUENCE

OTHER PEOPLE? HOW DO THEY MAKE THEM FEEL?
YOU WILL FIND THAT THE CHOICES YOU MAKE TO
PROMOTE WELL-BEING ARE MORE SUCCESSFUL THAN
CHOICES YOU MAKE OUT OF SELF-INTEREST. TO
BRING HAPPINESS AND LOVE INTO YOUR LIFE, YOU
NEED TO BRING THEM TO OTHERS. IF YOU DON'T SEE
AN IMMEDIATE RESULT FOR YOUR GOOD ACTIONS,
PATIENTLY WAIT, AND OBSERVE. BE CERTAIN THAT
BLESSINGS AND GIFTS GROW FROM YOUR GOOD
THOUGHTS AND ACTIONS. BE PREPARED TO LOOK AT
YOUR CHOICES IN LIFE AND HEAR THE MESSAGES I
HAVE TO GIVE YOU. COOPERATE WITH AND ENCOUR-
AGE YOUR DESTINY. ABOVE ALL, HAVE A PROFOUND
AND PERSONAL APPRECIATION OF THE MAGIC OF LIFE.
COMPREHEND YOUR MANY LIFETIMES AS A WHOLE
WHILE YOU DEEPLY FEEL THE IMPORTANCE OF THE
LIFE YOU ARE LIVING RIGHT NOW. ASK YOURSELF
WHAT IT IS THAT YOU TRULY LOVE TO DO. WHAT IS IT
THAT UPLIFTS AND INSPIRES YOU? WHAT IS IT YOU DO
THAT BRINGS MORE LOVE INTO YOUR LIFE AND INTO
THE LIVES OF OTHERS? IMAGINE WHAT IT IS IN LIFE
YOU ARE HERE TO DO. IMAGINE YOURSELF THE WAY
YOU WANT TO BE, DOING THE THINGS YOU LOVE TO
DO. THIS IS YOUR LIFE PURPOSE FOR THIS LIFETIME."

AS YOUR GUIDE SPEAKS, YOU BEGIN TO UNDER-
STAND WHAT YOU MUST DO IN THIS LIFETIME. YOU
BEGIN TO UNDERSTAND HOW TO DO WHAT YOU HAVE
SET OUT TO DO, THE ACTIONS YOU NEED TO TAKE.
YOU SUDDENLY HAVE THE INTUITIVE AWARENESS THAT

EVERYTHING IS JUST AS IT SHOULD BE IN THIS LIFE-
TIME. YOUR SPIRIT GUIDE CONTINUES SPEAKING:

"ALL IS TIMELESS. EXPERIENCE THE ONENESS OF
IT ALL. YOU ARE ETERNAL. UNDERSTAND THAT NOTH-
ING IS LOST, AND THAT EVERYONE AND EVERYTHING YOU
ARE AND HAVE BEEN IS RETAINED. AS A BEING OF
LIGHT, EVERY THOUGHT YOU HAVE AND ACTION YOU
MAKE MEANS THERE IS ANOTHER ACTION AND THOUGHT.
YOUR THOUGHTS AND ACTIONS ARE LIKE THE RIPPLES
IN A POOL. EVERYTHING FLOWS INTO EVERYTHING ELSE.
EVERYTHING RESPONDS TO EVERYTHING ELSE. WHAT
HAPPENS IN ONE PLACE AFFECTS WHAT HAPPENS IN
ANOTHER. EVERYTHING IS CONNECTED. ALL IS ONE."

YOU BEGIN TO UNDERSTAND DEEP WITHIN THAT
THERE IS NO SEPARATION, ONLY ONENESS. ALL REAL-
ITIES, ALL OF YOUR LIFETIMES, ARE MANIFESTATIONS
OF DIVINITY. YOU, TOO, ARE GODDESS AND GOD,
AND CAN CONNECT WITH YOUR DIVINE NATURE.

YOU REALIZE THAT YOU ARE NOT YOUR EGO. YOU
ARE NOT SEPARATE. YOU NO LONGER FEEL THE
NEED TO CREATE MORE KARMA BY SEEKING
REVENGE, GETTING EVEN, OR MAKING YOURSELF A
SELF-APPOINTED INSTRUMENT OF KARMA.

AS YOU REALIZE THESE THINGS AND MORE, YOUR
SPIRIT GUIDE MERGES HER OR HIS LIGHT WITH YOUR
OWN. YOU BECOME ONE AND THE SAME. AT THIS
TIME, ASK YOUR GUIDE ANY PRESSING QUESTIONS
YOU MAY HAVE. YOU WILL INTUITIVELY RECEIVE AN
ANSWER WITHIN YOU.

In this merged state with your spirit guide, you feel like a brilliant star of white light. As a star of bright light, you radiate divine love in all directions, sending healing thoughts and prayers of love to the world, to those people you care for, and to yourself in this lifetime and in all of your lifetimes.

Feel the love and healing energy flow from you and radiate back to you. Breathe it in, and breathe it out, shining its beaming light through time and space.

As you continue to breathe in the warm white light, you begin to realize that the positive events in your life, your joys and successes, just as negative ones, your disappointments and failures, are caused by your own actions and thoughts. They arise from choices made and experiences gained in this lifetime and other lifetimes. The responsibility is in your hands, and you cherish this knowledge. It helps you to understand, rather than struggle against, daily life.

As you continue to feel peaceful and calm, breathing slowly and quietly, you recognize that reality is not what lies outside of you; it is what lies within you. As your inner self changes awareness, you begin to perceive the outer world differently.

You begin to recognize that the material

WORLD IS MOLDED BY CONSCIOUSNESS. AS YOUR
CONSCIOUSNESS EXPANDS, YOU BEGIN TO MOLD
YOUR LIFE IN CREATIVE AND BALANCED WAYS. YOU
DISCOVER MORE LOVE AND HAPPINESS IN YOUR LIFE
BECAUSE YOU NOW KNOW WHAT IT IS YOU ARE HERE
TO DO, WHAT YOUR PURPOSE IS.

YOU DISCOVER THAT HAPPINESS IS YOUR NATURAL
STATE OF CONSCIOUSNESS, A STATE OF MIND THAT
SPRINGS FROM WITHIN. YOU FOCUS ON BRINGING
MORE LOVE INTO YOUR LIFE BY FOLLOWING YOUR
LIFE PURPOSE AND BALANCING YOUR MANY LIFE-
TIMES. YOU KNOW THAT YOU CAN NATURALLY
DEVELOP YOUR CAPACITY TO LOVE AND BE LOVED BY
OTHERS.

AS YOU BATHE IN THE STREAM OF FLOWING
WHITE LIGHT, FEEL IT REFRESH AND REVITALIZE YOU
COMPLETELY. DO THIS FOR A FEW MOMENTS.

FEELING STRONG AND FILLED WITH PURPOSE,
TAKE A DEEP BREATH THROUGH YOUR MOUTH, AND
EXHALE THROUGH YOUR NOSE. SLOWLY OPEN YOUR
EYES AND COME BACK TO YOUR WAKING CONSCIOUS-
NESS, MOVING YOUR HANDS AND FEET, WIGGLING
YOUR TOES AND FINGERS. NOW COME COMPLETELY
BACK TO THE PRESENT MOMENT BY CLAPPING YOUR
HANDS TOGETHER THREE TIMES.

☞ *When you are finished meditating, take a few
minutes to think about the feelings and thoughts that arose
within you. Make a few notes about your spirit guide, her*

or his name, and your life purpose, together with some of the steps you can take to balance your lifetimes.

It is important to recognize that the communication between yourself and your spirit guide can be very useful. Your guide provides guidance about your purpose as well as your other life patterns, so it is essential to thank her or him when you have received helpful information. Whenever you need more guidance and help, repeat this meditation, or simply call your guide by name and ask for the help that you need.

After your meditation experience, I suggest that you consider the following questions to fine-tune the process.

(Were you able to connect clearly with your guide?

(What were your impressions of your guide?

(How did you feel during the meditation?

(Did you learn anything of value, either about yourself, others, or the world during the meditation?

(How did you feel after the meditation?

CHAPTER FOUR

Future
Lifetimes

Is not almost all heaven filled with the human? Those very gods themselves had their origin here below, and ascended from hence into heaven.

Cicero

As Is the Past,
So Is the Future

In their book *Lives Unlimited: Reincarnation East and West*, H. N. Banerjee and Will Oursler report the case of William George, a fisherman who lived in Alaska. Although not a Tlingit himself, George was familiar with and accepted the native idea that the soul is immortal and lives on after the death of the physical body. He believed it so much so that he told his son, Reginald George, that if there was anything to the idea, he would come back and be Reginald's son. His son wondered how he would know that it was really William, and his father responded by pointing at two moles, one on his left shoulder and the other on his forearm. He told Reginald that these birthmarks would be the sign.

A little later, William once again brought up the subject of death and rebirth. At this time he gave Reginald his watch, telling his son to keep it for him. Reginald gave the watch to his wife, Susan. She put it in a jewelry box for safekeeping.

Several days afterward, William George went fishing as he usually did, but this time he did not return. Search parties searched but found nothing. It was concluded that William must have drowned. Then on May 5, 1950, almost nine months to the day that William disappeared, Reginald's wife, Susan, gave birth to a son, who displayed two prominent moles on his left shoulder and forearm, just like his grandfather. In addition, the mother, when she was in labor with the child, had dozed off and felt she had seen the image of William, her husband's father, just before she awoke and had the baby. Because of this, she insisted the boy be named William George II.

While growing up, William George II emulated his grandfather, William George, in several ways. These included walking in a manner that favored the right leg even though the boy had never injured his leg. His late grandfather had injured his right ankle. Because it never fully healed, he always walked in a way that favored his right leg.

William George II also resembled his grandfather in appearance. He had many of the same facial expressions and gestures. He even referred to his uncles and aunts on his father's side as his sons and daughters. On one occasion, William George II was present when his mother opened her jewelry box. Upon seeing and then picking up his grandfather's watch for the first time, he said that the watch was his. He steadfastly held on to this claim even after his mother took back the watch.

One reason the case of William George and William George II is significant is that it has the dual nature of being both a past life and a future life. From the vantage point of the grandson, the case represents a past life because the grandfather is a previous incarnation of the grandson. At the same time, from the vantage point of the grandfather, the case represents a future life because the grandson represents a future lifetime of the grandfather. This future lifetime was one that the grandfather predicted and possibly influenced through his intention to come back as his own grandson. This was clearly indicated by what he told his son before he died.

Multiple lifetimes within families as in the case of William George and William George II are fairly common. Many times, there exists an energetic bond between family members that can be especially strong; mothers and children, married couples, grandparents and grandchildren. Many of the proponents of past and future lives agree that people often seem to reincarnate in such a way as to be with their same family group. We tend to cluster together in lifetimes. This suggests that our intention can influence more than just our present lifetime. Perhaps our intention can also influence our future lifetimes, particularly when our intention is focused on the desired outcome—in this case, the future lifetime. This poses an interesting line of thought given the nature of the current research being done on energy fields that exist in and around the human body.

What this connection between lifetimes demonstrates is the direct correlation between past lives and future lives. If past lives exist on some level, then it is also probable that future lives are real on some level. This also suggests once again that the soul and spirit are immortal. They are eternal.

Daily life has a tendency to put a damper on the concept of spiritual immortality. For example, as a human being with a physical body, you often view things as being locked into this seemingly fixed reality. This is practical in many ways. You are born. You live and grow older, and eventually die.

Your soul and spirit exist outside the normal bounds of time and space, primarily because they are abstract in terms of this physical reality. They cannot be pinned down in physical time and space. Folks are still trying to put spirit under the microscope, trying to quantify and identify it. If only it were that easy. Instead, spirit and soul are like light dancing off the droplets of water in a rainbow—observable, beautiful, and divine.

Pushing the Historical Envelope

The concept of reincarnation, of past, present, and future lifetimes, in which time acts as a continuum—ever-beginning and never-ending—is no longer that far-fetched. After all, what was once considered fiction often becomes fact later in time.

One example of fiction into fact can be seen in the case of Galileo Galilei, born in 1564 as the son of a Florence nobleman. He was educated at the University of Pisa, and eventually became a professor of mathematics. Early on, he became interested in the ideas of Nicolas Copernicus, ideas that pushed against the accepted constraints of both science and religion of his day and age.

After reading about a Dutch astronomer who had made a crude telescope, Galileo made telescopes that were optically better. Because of this, he was able to better observe the movement of the planets and stars. He noticed that the planet Venus had phases much like those of the moon. From his careful observations, he concluded that Venus revolved around the Sun in an orbit inside that of the Earth.

Based on the teachings of Aristotle and other classical philosophers, the prevailing scientific belief at

Galileo's time was the Ptolemaic theory. Named after the Alexandrian philosopher and writer Claudius Ptolemy, this theory said that the Earth was a fixed planet. The Earth was an immovable mass at the center of the universe, meaning that everything, including the Sun and stars, moved around it. In addition, the universe was basically a spherical envelope outside of which there was nothing.

These ideas fit with the perspective on the universe held by the people of Galileo's time from the vantage point of the Earth, and the ideas fit with their egocentric assumption that human beings were the center of everything. This also matched the Christian religious doctrines at the time, which believed that people, as God's creation, were the hub of existence. Church philosopher Thomas Aquinas even showed that the scientific postulations of Aristotle and other Greek philosophers were in accordance with the church.

In 1633, when Galileo was an elderly man, he was brought before and tried by the Inquisition for crimes of heresy regarding his belief in the ideas of Copernicus, including that the Earth rotated on its axis once daily and traveled around the Sun once yearly. Under the threat of torture and death, he was forced on his knees to renounce all belief in Copernican theories. Galileo spent the rest of his life in prison, never allowed to publish any other works.

Although Galileo's sentence was horridly unjust, he fared better than his contemporary Giordano Bruno, who by the same Inquisition, was burned to death for his ideas. Bruno went so far as to suggest that space was boundless and that it contained many suns and solar systems. More than 400 years later, scientists, astronomers, and theologians all accept these theories as facts.

Beyond Ordinary Reality

Both reincarnation and time as a continuum are ideas that are abstract and move beyond the boundaries of what most think is "real." While writing this book, I asked several people what they thought of the idea of reincarnation. Some believed in reincarnation and were eager to talk about it. Some were curious, whereas others responded by saying it was "a bunch of malarkey."

In the past, Western religion and science have dismissed reincarnation as mostly fictional. The concept of reincarnation most definitely pushes the envelope of ordinary reality. Because of this, reincarnation is often dismissed in much the same way as Galileo and his Copernican ideas about the universe and Bruno and his concepts of space were dismissed.

The great dinosaurs lived long ago in an age far beyond present perception. This doesn't mean that they didn't exist. The stars in space are also outside our perception in the sense that it is yet impossible to hop into the nearest spaceship and go check them out in person. Yet, both dinosaur theory and star theory are based on observable evidence such as bones, fossils, DNA, and photographic and computer data, even though no one has actually touched a living dinosaur or set foot on a star.

Studying reincarnation is similar to studying dinosaurs and stars in that determinations are made on what the evidence suggests. Unfortunately, there is very little measurable data in reincarnation research. By nature, it is an observable phenomenon rather than a measurable one. In the Western world of the "show me" attitude, it is almost impossible to prove reincarnation using normal scientific methods.

Whether proven or not by standard scientific methods, the belief in reincarnation continues. It's much like the New Age motto "Metaphysics is not an option." In other words, it's happening all the while, whether you are aware of it or not. Metaphysics is part of the human experience. Things do go bump in the night—most every night, no matter what lifetime you are living. As more research is done and new discoveries are made, the theories regarding reincarnation can be adapted and modified accordingly. This is the nature of the evolution of human knowledge.

Time As a Continuum

A continuum is a coherent whole that is subdivided into minute parts. These minute parts progress through a succession of values or elements from one point to another. In the case of reincarnation, this progress is from the past to the future. Rather than being at the opposite ends of a line as in a linear time viewpoint, or even a circle where beginning meets the end, time is a holistic concept that can be observed and accessed at several levels of perception.

As a continuum, time is characteristically more spherical than linear. It is ever-beginning and never-ending, never-beginning and ever-ending. Time has neither a beginning nor an end, and is therefore infinite in nature and eternal in spirit. In this way, time is a paradox.

Because of its infinite nature, time suggests patterns that transcend the physical boundaries that most people accept as "real." These physical boundaries are practical when you need to get to a meeting on time, yet illusionary when you are exploring past and future lifetimes. In fact, the connection of past and future lifetimes suggests that all lives are happening simultaneously. Consider the possibility that there are a thousand yous, or even an infinite number of yous, all existing at the some moment in an infinite number of realms. This concept is being embraced by physicists, scientists, theologians, those in earth-spirited traditions, and New Agers alike. And it's not that far-fetched any longer. It's time to discover your thousand yous, to explore the possible lifetimes on which you can shine your light.

The main reason this lifetime seems more real is because of your vantage point. You are physically here in time and space, and perceive and sense your immediate reality from this orientation. You probably have already noticed that everything changes depending on your point of view.

Hypnosis is a useful tool in past life regression and future life progression because it can be used to alter your viewpoint. It puts you in an altered state of awareness in which time and space become malleable. Time and space become like a river, and your mind is the boat you use to navigate. By setting the boat on the waters, and tapping into your past and future lifetimes, you significantly alter your point of view in your daily life. It is also probable that you alter your point of view in your other lifetimes as well.

By perceiving life and all its many facets as multi-dimensional with overlappings and crystal-like inclusions, you realize perception is important. Within the context of time, perception becomes dynamic, meaning that it can be used to transport you to infinite lifetimes, changing your awareness of locality, circumstance, and state of mind.

Hypnosis, ritual, nature quests, drumming, dancing, chanting, intense emotion, eating certain foods, daydreaming, making love, and dreaming can all be used to alter the state or tense (the temporal sense) of your mind. In this different state, you move your awareness one step beyond ordinary reality and through the door into oneness. While in this different state of mind, you can perceive your many lifetimes. Often this is experienced as a flashing image of a lifetime. It is in this different state of mind that you can more readily connect with the divine—the divine within and without. In this way, past life regression and future life progression can act as agents of powerful change in your spiritual growth.

Life has many aspects to it, many of which we obviously still don't understand, and still others we have yet to conceive. These aspects definitely include death and reincarnation. What we do know about death and reincarnation strongly suggests that time is a continuum rather than a linear concept. Certain energetic patterns such as the soul, and connections with other souls, seem to continue on. The past and future are forever a part of each other and become timeless in nature. All is one. The idea of separation comes from our perception. It comes from being thrust into a seemingly separate physical body and cut off from our mothers. Then the separation grows stronger as we sense and question the physical world into which we are born. Although practical, this perceived separation cuts us off from our divinity and our many selves.

Time Travel

It's probable that we will discover new ways to prove (or disprove) reincarnation—for instance, with time travel. H. G. Wells's novel (and popular film) *The Time Machine* begins with the Time Traveller talking with his well-educated friends about the possibility of time travel. He concludes the discussion by unveiling a small object. He points out that the little machine is only a model of a larger machine he plans to build that can travel through time. Showing them two white levers on the apparatus, the Time Traveller says,

> *Now I want you clearly to understand that this lever, being pressed over, sends the machine gliding into the future, and this other reverses the motion. This saddle represents the seat of a time traveller. Presently I am going to press the lever,*

*and off the machine will go. It will vanish, pass
into future Time, and disappear. Have a good look
at the thing. Look at the table too, and satisfy
yourselves there is no trickery. I don't want to
waste this model, and then be told I'm a quack.*

The Time Traveller starts to push the lever, but stops and turns to the psychologist in the group, taking his hand in his own. He tells the psychologist to stick out his forefinger, and so it is the psychologist's touch that sends the model time machine on its interminable voyage. Everyone watches the lever turn and no trickery is evident. Wells writes,

*There was a breath of wind, and the lamp flame
jumped. One of the candles on the mantel was
blown out, and the little machine suddenly swung
round, became indistinct, was seen as a ghost for
a second perhaps, as an eddy of faintly glittering
brass and ivory; and it was gone—vanished! Save
for the lamp the table was bare.*

The basic principles of Wells's time machine contain materials that regard time as the fourth dimension. At the time the book was published, this idea was in opposition to the prevailing Newtonian theory of time and space, but at the same time very much in accordance with the later theories of Albert Einstein, who postulated the four-dimensional continuum of space—time.

Much like Ptolemy's theories regarding the solar system, Newton's theories based themselves around the notion that time and space are absolute, and in this sense there is a single fixed time that is symbolized by an imaginary clock somewhere in space that keeps everything right on time.

Like Copernicus and Galileo, Einstein sought answers that pushed the envelope of the accepted boundaries of traditional scientific thought. Time and space are curved, and gravity is the movement of matter along the shortest distance in curved space and time. What Einstein said in effect was that time is what a clock reads, whether it is the rotation of a planet, a heartbeat, or sand falling in an hourglass.

Time is relative to the context in which it is perceived. This means that everyone and everything exhibiting the powers of awareness perceive time a little differently. No one is having the exact same experience with time. This includes people, animals, birds, insects, trees, plants, and so forth.

By its nature, reincarnation moves beyond the space and time continuum into a different realm of space and time. When you move beyond the space and time continuum, you release your attachment to your physical body. Many accounts exist of people talking about near-death and other out-of-body experiences that transport them beyond this time and space. In one particular account, a woman who had been blind since birth had an out-of-body experience in which she could see. To this person, her experience was very real, and it permanently changed her point of view about her present lifetime.

Visionaries and Psychics

With a suggestion, for example in hypnosis, you can tap into some form of a future lifetime that you may experience. As such it gives you momentary images of the future, not just your future, but the future of the planet as well. There have been some visionaries and psychics who have tapped into the future patterns with remarkable accuracy, well beyond scientific probability.

Born February 8, 1828, in the French seaport city of Nantes, Jules Verne set out at the age of twenty to follow in his father's footsteps as an attorney. At college in Paris, he diligently completed his study of law. Instead of being interested in law when he completed his studies, he was drawn to the Parisian literary world.

Encouraged by his friend and mentor, Alexandre Dumas, author of the classic book *The Three Musketeers*, Verne began writing poems and plays. While working at the Theatre Lyrique, he also began writing science articles for a local magazine. These articles required hours of research in the library. As he was doing this research, he had the inspiration for a "novel of science" that mixed scientific fact in a fictional story format.

In 1862, Verne met publisher Pierre Hetzel, who suggested a style that was fast-paced adventure coupled with a scientific visionary manner and an optimistic outlook toward the role of technology in the world.

This outlook differed from Verne's own viewpoints, which he expressed more frequently after Hetzel's death in

1886. These views are poignantly expressed in a recently discovered manuscript that describes Paris in the twentieth century as having skyscrapers of glass and steel, high-speed trains, gas-powered automobiles, calculators, fax machines, and a global communications network. He describes it as a future in which people struggle to find happiness in a world that has become materialistic. In addition, he thought people should respect the environment and be more socially responsible.

Through time, Verne wrote more than sixty novels, starting with *Five Weeks in a Balloon* in 1863. The next year he wrote *Journey to the Center of the Earth*, a story that has been immortalized several times in movie form. In 1865, as the American Civil War was ending, he published *From the Earth to the Moon*, which contains many similarities to the actual *Apollo 11* moon mission that happened 104 years later. The three that stand out are the following:

1. *The launching site in Verne's book was not that far from Cape Canaveral, the actual launching site.*
2. *Verne gave the correct initial velocity required for a spaceship to escape the Earth's gravity.*
3. *In the sequel book,* Around the Moon, *Verne describes weightlessness in space and the problems experienced with reentry into the Earth's atmosphere. The reentry Verne describes in his book happens in the Pacific Ocean and is three miles from where* Apollo 11 *landed on its return from the moon in 1969.*

The coincidences here are extraordinary, to say the least. When this occurs, something else is going on, something out of the ordinary that can't be explained in a logical manner. In this case, Verne was obviously glimpsing patterns in the future, very real patterns that came about. He gave his writing a lot of thought. He meditated on it, so to speak. It's also likely that he went over passages and scenes he was writing again and again, merging with them and becoming one with them as if they were real. By doing so, he was able to create an even more detailed glimpse of future life on our planet.

Wells, like Verne, tapped into the future. Because of his vividly accurate depictions of the twentieth century, he is often referred to as "the man who invented tomorrow." His visions of the future included superhighways, overcrowded cities, computers, videocassette players, television, and the atomic bomb. He said that if we did not change, we would destroy ourselves. In Wells's vision of the future, there is cataclysmic world war. Afterward a visionary elite take over. He wrote that by the middle of the twenty-first century, the world would be at peace, and we would enjoy the fruits of technology.

Like the past life experiences that are meticulously researched by Dr. Ian Stevenson, the works of Wells and Verne check out. After all, we do have submarines, spaceships, overcrowded cities, television, computers, a global information system, and so forth. From this data, questions naturally arise. For instance, Was it the perceptions and writing of these two visionary authors that brought about these things? Or were they simply tapping into future patterns and lifetimes?

Authors and creative artists often say they are divinely inspired. Isn't that also true in terms of writing about the future as shown in visionary fiction? And if so, does the future take its form from this divine inspiration? Does fiction become fact through human thought and action, or was it fact all along? All these questions have many answers, yet none of them are truly satisfactory. At the same time, these questions all need to be asked if we are to advance our understanding of death, reincarnation, future patterns, and future lifetimes.

The influence of visionary artists continues much beyond their physical lives on this plane. For instance, influential people who cite Verne's influence on their accomplishments include Neil Armstrong, the first person to walk on the Moon, Admiral Richard Byrd, Antarctica explorer, and Yuri Gagarin, the first person to fly in space. Many say that without Verne's visions of the future, this world would be a much different place, and certain scientific discoveries would have taken longer, or possibly taken different courses.

Visionaries such as Verne and Wells see and influence events far beyond their own lives. As with life, the future is about probability and being in the right place at the right time. If the probability is high that you are in the right place at the right time, then the chances for success increase because there are fewer odds that you have to overcome.

Other visionary fiction writers such as Aldus Huxley, George Orwell, Ursula LeGuin, Arthur C. Clark, Frank Herbert, and Kurt Vonnegut, and filmmaker George Lucas also create future worlds. The future world that Lucas creates, for example, has a power that connects all life together. As you master this power or life force, you become a master of, rather than a pawn in, your own destiny and fate.

Many filmmakers have created films, just as many visionary fiction authors have written stories, about what will happen in the future. Their ability to tap into the future is often uncanny and akin to the idea of future lives in that they seem to move a part of their awareness into the future, and then write or make a film about it.

Like the many visionary authors and filmmakers, you have the power to tap into and merge with the patterns of the future. By doing so, you can glimpse your future lifetimes. It is something you can easily master. A simple method is to hold a clear quartz crystal in your receiving hand (left hand if you are right-handed) as you are drifting to sleep. As you fall asleep, repeat to yourself, "I am dreaming through time and space into the future, and I will remember when I wake up." When you wake up, write down everything you recall from your dreams. Hold the stone in your receiving hand as you do this to trigger more complete recall. Repeat this process until you get the desired results.

The Visions
of Edgar Cayce

Edgar Cayce stands out as one of the most remarkable visionaries of our time. He was a photographer by trade, who from an early age was able to use out-of-body experiences in real life experiences. His mother told the story of how Edgar's father was going to punish him because he had not done his spelling homework. Edgar pleaded with his father to let him go to sleep for five minutes on the spelling book, saying that upon waking, he would know all the words. After much convincing, the father let Edgar go to sleep on the book for five minutes. After the boy awoke, he correctly spelled each word in the book, cover-to-cover. Understandably, he was not punished.

Two questions immediately come up regarding Cayce's method of spelling that don't fit with the normal ideas of time and space. First, how did he learn all the words by sleeping? And second, how did he do it all in five minutes? The answers can be found in the techniques and methods of Cayce, who is often called The Sleeping Prophet.

Cayce applied his out-of-body, "sleeping" skill as a medical intuitive. He successfully told people what was wrong with them and how to cure their ailments. At first because of his devout Christian background, he was reluctant to delve into past lives. Once during a reading, though, someone asked him about "the other side," which prompted Cayce to begin talking about the basics of reincarnation, including life after life and karma.

Cayce often found the root of medical or physical problems related to spiritual sources that could be directly traced to a past life. The remarkable thing was how amazingly accurate he was in his diagnoses. This becomes particularly glaring since he never came into contact with a patient before a reading. Instead, he went into a hypnotic state in another room, and then examined the patient by moving out of body and into the room where the patient sat waiting.

Cayce described his technique as changing his vibration of matter and moving into the giant library of the Akashic Records. This was a giant database filled with information about everything and anything—past, present, and future. "Akasha" is the Sanskrit word that describes the fundamental etheric, electro-spiritual substance of the universe. Every sound, movement, light, thought, action, and dream is impressed upon the Akashic Records. It's like a huge video camera of the universe. Cayce referred to it as the book of life and the universal memory of nature.

By tapping into the Akashic Records, Cayce did not need to confine his readings to present ailments and past lives, but could also do future life readings as a way to facilitate the healing of present illnesses.

Like Nostradamus, Cayce correctly predicted much of what is happening in the world today, from conflict in the Middle East to global warming. The implications from the work of visionaries such as Cayce is that tapping into the future is possible. By following certain methods and using specific techniques such as hypnosis, the past and the future may be accessible to many of us just as it was to him.

Some scientists now suggest the existence of wormholes that enable energy to travel great distances in extremely short periods of time. They are like time and space portals. These wormholes have also been suggested as possible avenues into what Cayce coined as the Akashic Record, or what Carl Jung termed the "collective unconsciousness." Now we just have to figure out how to successfully tap into and find, enter, and exit these time and space wormholes.

A Case of Future Life Progression

In his book *Past Lives, Future Lives*, Dr. Bruce Goldberg describes the case of a man named Harry. Harry had already gone through a number of past life regressions, so he was familiar with the basic process.

Goldberg began by progressing Harry a week into the future at a time. Because Harry's job was related to the news, Goldberg asked him to read what was going to be in the news in the next week. This type of progression was done on several occasions, and out of the six news items that Harry read from the future, four occurred on the day he had said. One of the news events happened three days before and another happened five days earlier. The statistical odds of this occurring just by guessing are completely off the charts. Although it doesn't prove the validity and practicality of future life progressions, it does suggest there is something more going on, something extraordinary that can possibly be mastered, given enough practice.

In a later session, Goldberg progressed Harry to a lifetime in the future. In this lifetime, Harry lives and works in a glass pyramid being used for farming purposes. In this futuristic world, food is grown by hydroponics, computers oversee the operation of most everything, and people communicate by the power of thought. In Harry's description of the end of this future life, he goes into a termination room. In this room is a device that Harry is hooked up to that takes his energy from him. In Harry's future world, humans are still biological, but they no longer grow old. Instead they are transferred into new bodies. During the in-between lifetimes, a person's energetic patterns are stored on a kind of tape until her or his next reincarnation.

Moving Forward in Time

The concept of future life progression is basically the same as past life regression. The main difference is that instead of moving your awareness into your past life patterns, you move your awareness forward into your future life patterns. You move your awareness from your present lifetime into the in-between time. From this in-between time, you select and move your awareness into a future lifetime. When you are finished exploring your future lifetime, you move your awareness back into the in-between time, and then back into the present time and space. You move your awareness, not your body.

As with past lives, future lives can help you better understand aspects of yourself and the world around you. The people who are visionaries and psychics are those who can move beyond this present reality into the worlds of the future. The future is connected to the past on a physical and energetic level at the moment the present happens. In terms of healing, this means that future healings affect perceptions of past lives, and thus can give healing benefits in your present life. In this sense, the source of healing energy is timeless.

As people, we suggest the possibility of a human continuum that reflects the tendencies of time and space. Nothing truly dies, but instead harmonically changes with relation to our perception, which is keyed into particular rates of vibration. We move through multiple lives that stretch out through our perceived past and future. These lives are a direct reflection of one another, and affect one another in a variety of ways because of their connection in the dimension of time.

In terms of the general theory of relativity, your perception depends on your "reference frame." Each frame gives a different perception, depending on the manner in which you move through the universe. In terms of reincarnation, the view from future lives is much different than the view from past lives. Each view gives you a more complete look at the totality of your life—where you have been, where you are, and where you are going.

By better understanding the interconnected nature of all things within the whole, you become better aware of your divine nature. If the human soul is indeed immortal, then it's a little like the Bill Murray character in the movie *Groundhog Day*: It's just a matter of eventually getting it right, starting with where you are right now, here today. Change is enacted in sequences from the small to the large—step-by-step, day-by-day, lifetime-by-lifetime.

Life creates patterns, whether past, present, or future, ultimately all connected together into oneness. This one-ness is boundless, timeless, and waits to be experienced by each participant who makes up its whole. It is essentially a divine database you can learn to tap into.

Future Life Meditation

This future life meditation can be used to tap into that divine database and help you explore your future lifetimes. It gives you an opportunity to view your life patterns from the future. Gaining insight into the future and where you are going can help give you insights into your present lifetime.

To get the most out of this progression I suggest that you tape-record it in your own voice. Then play it back whenever you want to explore your future lifetimes. This is something you can do again and again. I have yet to run out of lifetimes, either in my own case or when progressing others. Each time you use this meditation, the experience expands your awareness.

If you prefer, have your partner or a close friend slowly read the meditation to you, allowing sufficient time for you to experience the journey. You can also read the progression to yourself, following along a paragraph at a time, but using a tape recording of it is preferable. You can become more relaxed using a tape recording. This assures a deeper and more vivid future life experience. (See pages 4 and 5 for tips on reading the meditations.)

Be sure you are not interrupted when doing this meditation. Turn on the answering machine and turn the volume off. Put pets and electronic devices such as your cell phone out of the room to avoid interruptions.

Meditation

BEGIN BY SITTING, RECLINING, OR LYING BACK COMFORTABLY. LOOSEN ANY CLOTHING, BELTS, TIES, OR SHOES THAT MIGHT BE TIGHT AND BINDING YOU. JUST GET AS COMFORTABLE AS YOU CAN. UNCROSS YOUR ARMS AND LEGS AND TAKE A FEW DEEP BREATHS, SETTLING AND SINKING INTO THE SURFACE BENEATH YOU A LITTLE BIT MORE WITH EACH BREATH.

CONTINUE TO BREATHE DEEPLY AND CLOSE YOUR EYES. AS YOU BREATHE IN, MOVE YOUR EYES UPWARD, WITHOUT OPENING THEM. THEN AS YOU BREATHE OUT, MOVE YOUR EYES DOWNWARD, WITHOUT OPENING THEM. CONTINUE DOING THIS FOR SEVERAL BREATHS.

NOW AS YOU BREATHE IN, IMAGINE BREATHING IN SOOTHING WHITE LIGHT. AS YOU EXHALE, IMAGINE

LETTING GO OF ALL THE TENSIONS AND WORRIES OF THE DAY. LET GO AND ALLOW YOUR BODY TO COMPLETELY RELAX, RELEASING ALL THE TENSION IN YOUR MUSCLES WITH EACH BREATH.

BREATHE THE SOOTHING WHITE LIGHT INTO YOUR HEAD, AND THEN SLOWLY IMAGINE THE SOOTHING WHITE LIGHT FILLING YOUR FACE AND NECK, AND MOVING OVER AND THROUGH YOUR SHOULDERS, RELAXING YOU EVEN MORE. TAKE A DEEP BREATH AND DROP YOUR SHOULDERS AS YOU EXHALE.

BREATHE THE SOOTHING WHITE LIGHT INTO YOUR ARMS, HANDS, AND FINGERS, AND THEN INTO YOUR CHEST, BACK, AND STOMACH. KEEP BREATHING THE SOOTHING WHITE LIGHT INTO YOUR PELVIS AND BUTTOCKS, AND THEN INTO YOUR THIGHS, KNEES, CALVES, ANKLES, FEET, AND TOES.

NOW BREATHE IN FOR THREE HEARTBEATS, HOLD YOUR BREATH FOR THREE HEARTBEATS, AND EXHALE FOR THREE HEARTBEATS. KEEP BREATHING THIS WAY, RELAXING MORE AND MORE, DEEPER AND DEEPER, BECOMING MORE PEACEFUL AND RELAXED. AFTER YOU BREATHE THIS WAY FOR A COUPLE OF MINUTES, YOU MAY FIND THAT YOUR BODY FEELS AS THOUGH IT IS BREATHING ITSELF, NATURALLY, KNOWING, TRUSTING, REMEMBERING THAT FEELING OF SERENITY AND HARMONY.

IN YOUR MIND'S EYE, IMAGINE BEING IN A MAGICAL FOREST. MIGHTY OAKS, GIANT ASH TREES, AND TOWERING SUGAR PINES SURROUND YOU. YOU

CAN HEAR BIRDS IN THE TREE CANOPY AND THE
SOUND OF WATER RUNNING INTO A MOUNTAIN LAKE
THAT STRETCHES OUT BEFORE YOU. THERE IS A
SMALL ISLAND WITH SEVERAL LARGE TREES IN THE
MIDDLE OF THE LAKE. AS YOU GAZE OUT TOWARD
THE ISLAND, THE FRESH SCENT OF THE TREES,
EARTH, AND WATER WASHES OVER YOU, CARRIED ON
A SOFT BREEZE. THE BREEZE ECHOES IN THE TREES,
CREATING A SOFT WAVE OF SOUND THAT WEAVES IN
AND OUT OF THE FOREST, AGAIN AND AGAIN.

A THICK WHITE FOG ROLLS OVER THE LAKE AND
FLOWS TOWARD YOU. IT FILLS THE WOODS ALL
AROUND YOU, SHINING SILVER AND GOLD AS THE
SUN'S RAYS SLICE THROUGH IT. THE GLISTENING MIST
BRUSHES AGAINST YOUR LEGS LIKE A PURRING CAT,
AND THEN IT SLOWLY SURROUNDS AND ENFOLDS
YOU. THE FOG FEELS ODDLY RELAXING AND FAMILIAR
AS IT GENTLY SWIRLS OVER YOUR FEET AND LEGS, UP
YOUR THIGHS, TORSO, OVER YOUR LIMBS, AND UP
OVER YOUR SHOULDERS, OVER AND THROUGH YOUR
HEAD. THE FOG FILLS THE SPACE ABOVE AND BELOW
YOU, BEFORE, BESIDE, AND BEHIND YOU. YOU CAN
FEEL ITS MOISTURE COOLING YOUR FACE. YOU CAN
EVEN TASTE THE TINY DROPLETS OF DEW WITHIN THE
SHINING MIST.

THE FOG GROWS THICKER AND MORE CLOUDLIKE,
AND YOU FEEL AS THOUGH YOU ARE FLOATING IN
THE FOREST. YOU FEEL AS THOUGH YOU ARE BEING
LIFTED ON A WHITE CLOUD AND SAILING THROUGH

THE WOODS LIKE A BOAT CUTTING THROUGH THE
WATER.

IN THE NEXT INSTANT, YOU FIND YOURSELF IN A
MAGICAL SAILBOAT ON THE LAKE. THE BOAT MOVES
ON ITS OWN ACCORD, AND FERRIES YOU ACROSS THE
MOUNTAIN LAKE TO THE MYSTERIOUS ISLAND. THE
SOFT BREEZE FILLS THE SAILS OF THE MAGICAL
VESSEL, AND THE BOAT MOVES FASTER AND FASTER
THROUGH THE FOG TOWARD THE SMALL ISLAND IN
THE MIDDLE OF THE LAKE.

AS YOU TRAVEL IN THE MAGICAL VESSEL, FACES
MADE OF HOLOGRAPHIC-LIKE ENERGY FLASH BRIEFLY
THROUGH YOUR AWARENESS. YOU ARE AWARE OF
THE FACES OF PEOPLE YOU HAVE KNOWN IN YOUR
PRESENT LIFETIME, FACES OF BOTH LIVING PEOPLE
AND THOSE WHO HAVE PASSED ON. YOU SENSE
THEIR PRESENCE FOR A MOMENT OR TWO AS YOU
SAIL ON TOWARD THE ISLAND.

A BRILLIANT WHITE LIGHT STREAMS ACROSS THE
LAKE. THE LIGHT STREAMS ACROSS THE BOAT, AND
YOU SAIL RIGHT THROUGH IT. AS YOU DO, IT FEELS
AS THOUGH YOU SAIL THROUGH A WINDOW OF LIGHT
INTO ANOTHER DIMENSION OF TIME AND SPACE. YOU
ARE NEITHER HERE NOR THERE, BUT AFLOAT IN SOME
TIMELESS OTHERWORLD.

YOU FEEL THE MAGICAL VESSEL NUDGE THE
ISLAND SHORE, AND IT REMAINS STATIONARY,
ANCHORED BY SOME UNSEEN HAND. YOU SLOWLY
STEP OUT OF THE BOAT AND WALK INLAND,

FOLLOWING AN EARTHEN PATH CUT THROUGH THE PINES AND UNDERBRUSH.

THE WHITE FOG AROUND YOU BEGINS TO CLEAR AS YOU WALK DOWN THE PATH. THE LAST OF THE WHITE FOG SHIMMERS IN THE SUN'S RAYS, BRIEFLY TWINKLES, AND THEN DISAPPEARS ALTOGETHER IN THE SOFT BREEZE, UNVEILING THE MAGICAL ISLAND ALL AROUND YOU.

YOU SEE A LARGE OAK TREE IN FRONT OF YOU. STANDING IN FRONT OF THE TREE IS AN ELDERLY WOMAN WITH A TIMELESS BEAUTY, DRESSED ALL IN WHITE. HER WHITE HAIR IS LONG AND HANGS DOWN ALMOST TO HER FEET. IN HER HANDS, SHE HOLDS A SMALL, CLEAR CRYSTAL WHEEL. SHE SMILES AT YOU AS YOU APPROACH HER. SHE EXTENDS HER HAND TO SHAKE YOURS, AND FIVE RAYS OF BRILLIANT WHITE LIGHT STREAM FROM HER FINGERS. SHAKING HER HAND FEELS LIKE SHAKING HANDS WITH THE SUN, WARM AND BRIGHT.

THE WOMAN IN WHITE HANDS THE WHEEL OUT FOR YOU TO HOLD. YOU TAKE THE WHEEL FROM HER. IT SEEMS TO HUM IN YOUR HANDS. YOU SLOWLY TURN IT CLOCKWISE, AND AS YOU DO THIS, YOU ARE SUDDENLY TRANSPORTED INTO A PORTAL IN THE FUTURE, INTO ONE OF YOUR LIFETIMES, IN PARTICULAR THE FUTURE LIFETIME THAT IS MOST APPROPRIATE FOR YOU TO EXPLORE RIGHT NOW.

AS YOU STEP INTO YOUR MOST APPROPRIATE FUTURE LIFETIME, YOU BEGIN TO LOOK AROUND.

NOTICE WHERE YOU ARE. DOES THE LAND LOOK FAMILIAR? WHAT PLANET ARE YOU ON? IS IT THE EARTH OR ANOTHER PLANET? WHAT DOES THE SKY LOOK LIKE? HOW MANY SUNS ARE IN THE SKY? ARE YOU BREATHING AIR OR SOMETHING ELSE? PERHAPS YOU AREN'T ON LAND AT ALL. IF NOT, WHERE ARE YOU?

NOW TAKE A FEW MOMENTS AND IN YOUR MIND'S EYE LOOK DOWN AT YOUR FEET, YOUR LEGS, STOMACH, ARMS, AND HANDS. ARE YOU FEMALE OR MALE, HUMAN OR OTHERWISE? PERHAPS YOU ARE PURE LIGHT AND HAVE NO PHYSICAL BODY.

BREATHE DEEPLY AND COMPLETELY, AND RELAX A LITTLE MORE. NOW SLOWLY IN YOUR MIND'S EYE NOTICE WHAT KIND OF CLOTHING YOU ARE WEARING, AND INDEED, WHETHER YOU ARE WEARING CLOTHING AT ALL. ALSO NOTICE THE COLOR OF YOUR SKIN. IF YOU DON'T SEEM TO HAVE SKIN, THEN NOTICE WHAT COVERS YOUR BODY.

NOW IN YOUR MIND'S EYE, BEGIN TO TAKE NOTICE OF THE OTHERS AROUND YOU. WHAT DO THESE PEOPLE OR BEINGS LOOK LIKE? WHAT ARE THEY DOING? ARE THEY ENGAGED IN ANY SPECIFIC ACTIVITY? ARE YOU? BEGIN TO INTERACT WITH THE OTHERS AROUND YOU. WHAT KIND OF COMMUNITY ARE YOU IN? DO THE OTHERS WELCOME AND KNOW YOU WELL, OR DO THEY SEEM LIKE STRANGERS?

FIND OUT WHAT YOUR NAME IS IN THIS LIFETIME. IF YOU DON'T RECALL YOUR NAME, ASK SOMEONE

CLOSE TO YOU WHAT YOUR NAME IS. MAKE A
MENTAL NOTE OF IT. ALSO ASK THE OTHERS AROUND
YOU WHAT THEIR NAMES ARE. MAKE MENTAL NOTES
OF THEM. ASK WHERE YOU ARE IF YOU DON'T KNOW.
MAKE AN EFFORT TO FIND OUT WHAT YEAR IT IS.
ASK THE OTHERS ANYTHING AND EVERYTHING YOU
MAY WANT TO KNOW, AND PAY CLOSE ATTENTION TO
THE ANSWERS YOU RECEIVE.

FOCUS ON WHO YOU HAVE CLOSE RELATIONSHIPS
WITH IN THIS OTHER LIFETIME. WHO ARE YOUR
MOTHER AND FATHER? TAKE A FEW MOMENTS AND
SEE YOUR PARENTS IN THIS FUTURE LIFETIME. WHAT
ARE THEIR MAIN QUALITIES? DO YOU HAVE CHILDREN,
AND IF SO, WHO ARE THEY AND WHAT ARE THEIR
MAIN QUALITIES? ARE YOU MARRIED? WHAT KIND OF
LOVE RELATIONSHIPS DO YOU HAVE IN THIS LIFETIME?

NOW TAKE A FEW MOMENTS AND IN YOUR MIND'S
EYE NOTICE THE KINDS OF DAILY ACTIVITIES IN WHICH
YOU ARE ENGAGED. NOTICE WHETHER YOU ENJOY
YOUR WORK AND WHAT YOU SPEND YOUR TIME
DOING. TAKE A FEW MOMENTS AND MOVE YOUR
AWARENESS FORWARD IN TIME. SEE YOUR LIFE
THROUGH THE YEARS, THE GOOD TIMES AND THE
BAD TIMES. MOVE YOUR AWARENESS FORWARD A
YEAR, THEN FIVE YEARS, AND THEN TEN YEARS.
MOVE YOUR AWARENESS FORWARD TWENTY YEARS,
THIRTY YEARS, AND THEN SLOWLY FORWARD TO THE
END OF THIS FUTURE LIFETIME.

TAKE A DEEP BREATH. AS YOU EXHALE, LET GO

OF ANY PAIN, HURT, AND ANY OTHER NEGATIVE FEELINGS FROM THIS FUTURE LIFETIME. DO THIS SEVERAL TIMES TO RID YOUR BEING OF ANY NEGATIVE RESIDUE.

NOW TAKE ANOTHER DEEP BREATH, AND AS YOU DO, FOCUS ON THE MANY POSITIVE EXPERIENCES IN THIS FUTURE LIFETIME: THE LOVE, JOY, PLEASURE, HAPPINESS, ENTHUSIASM, INSPIRATION, KINDNESS, AND EXCITEMENT. BREATHE THESE POSITIVE QUALITIES INTO YOUR BEING FROM THIS FUTURE LIFETIME. BRING THEM INTO YOUR BEING AS YOU BREATHE THEM IN AND FEEL THE POWER OF THE FUTURE STRENGTHEN YOU. MAKE A MENTAL NOTE OF THE SINGLE-MOST IMPORTANT THING YOU LEARNED FROM THIS FUTURE LIFETIME.

NOW ONCE AGAIN, IMAGINE BEING SURROUNDED BY THE THICK WHITE FOG. ALLOW IT TO ROLL OVER YOU, FILLING AND SOOTHING YOU COMPLETELY. THE SOFT WHITE MIST REFRESHES YOU, AND YOU FEEL REVITALIZED AND IN HARMONY. YOU EASILY AND READILY REMEMBER THE MANY DETAILS FROM YOUR FUTURE LIFE EXPLORATION. AS YOU BATHE IN THE SOOTHING WHITE FOG FOR A FEW MOMENTS, YOU CONTINUE TO RECALL MORE DETAILS FROM YOUR FUTURE LIFETIME EXPERIENCE.

NOW BEGIN TO RETURN YOUR AWARENESS TO THE PRESENT TIME AND PLACE. BRING YOUR AWARENESS BACK TO THE ROOM, MOVING YOUR LEGS, FEET, AND TOES. START TO MOVE YOUR ARMS,

HANDS, AND FINGERS, AND STRETCH A LITTLE, SHIFT-
ING YOUR BODY. FINALLY, RETURN COMPLETELY TO
YOUR BODY AND TO THE PRESENT TIME AND PLACE.

NEXT, SLOWLY OPEN YOUR EYES WITHOUT REALLY
FOCUSING ON ANYTHING IN PARTICULAR. THEN BEGIN
TO FOCUS AND TAKE A FEW MINUTES TO FULLY
STRETCH YOUR ARMS AND LEGS. AS YOU DO THIS,
THINK ABOUT YOUR FUTURE LIFE EXPLORATION.

☞ *Write down as many details as you can recall
about your future life exploration. You may find these notes
not only fascinating, but also invaluable in your present
lifetime. A shifting occurs when you begin exploring your
many selves, an empowering shift of expanding awareness
that permanently changes your perspective.*

CHAPTER FIVE

Personal
Evolution

We can make our lives sublime
And, departing, leave behind us
Footprints on the sands of time

Henry Wadsworth Longfellow, "Resignation"

Understanding
Your Lifetimes

Charles Spiegel, in his article "Past-Life Therapy—The New Psychiatry," describes the following case. A patient came to him whom medical doctors had given a diagnosis of schizophrenia. Descriptions indicated that the young man would function for a few months without any problems, but then would seem to fly off the handle and begin screaming what sounded like religious phrases. His erratic behaviors frightened the people around him so much that his parents had him locked up several times in mental institutions, where drugs were administered to him until the episodes ended. In this condition, he was not a functioning person.

The therapist regressed the patient into a past life in which he remembered being imprisoned, tortured, and eventually burned at the stake by the Inquisition. Interestingly, each autumn when the patient was arrested, he would play out the sequences of his trial, including the religious condemnations of his captors. Every February, his condition disappeared because he was executed in the past life at this time, thus ending the whole episode.

After undergoing the past life regression, the patient began dealing with his problems on a much different level. Now, he earns his livelihood as a printer and is a functioning person.

The above case is particularly significant because the patient was able to derive so much personal value from revisiting a past experience. Whether or not the overall concepts of reincarnation and past lives are real, there is definitely therapeutic value for some individuals who undergo the experience. This therapeutic, healing value is what makes understanding your lifetimes beneficial in terms of your present lifetime.

The Healing Benefits of Reincarnation

In her book *Return from Heaven*, Carol Bowman describes a case involving a woman named Kathy, who at sixteen had a son named James. The baby had curly blond hair and a delightfully good nature. With the father long gone and no family support, Kathy raised the baby on her own. At sixteen months, James received a diagnosis of a tumoral cancer. While dealing with the disease, doctors placed an IV in the right side of his neck, leaving a scar. Later on he developed a tumor behind his left eye that blinded him. He always told his mother not to cry, even on the day before he died.

Being so young and filled with grief, Kathy put the whole experience behind her. She found someone she cared about and had several other children. Her second child was delivered by cesarean section. While she was still drugged, the doctors told her that her son had no color in his left eye, and as a result was blind in that eye. Also when she first saw her son, whom she named Chad, she noticed a small birthmark that looked like an incision on the right side of his neck. He also had a cyst on his right side just where the doctors had removed the tissue for James's biopsy. The coincidences were mounting.

As he grew older, Chad walked by throwing his left leg outward in a motion that favored the right leg, just as James had done because of medical reasons. Upon examination, doctors could find no medical reason for the blindness in Chad's left eye. Also, when he was four, Chad asked his mother about their other house, the one that was orange and brown on the outside with chocolate-colored furniture on the inside. He also asked about a red "weeble-wobble" toy that jangled when it rolled. When Kathy asked Chad about why he wanted to go back to this other house, he replied by looking her straight in the eye and saying, "Because I left you there."

What astonished Kathy, who was raised as a Baptist with no prior knowledge of past lives or reincarnation, is that the other place Chad described was an orange and brown stucco apartment that she had lived in when James was a baby. The furniture was chocolate-colored and James had a toy like the one Chad remembered. Chad had never seen the apartment before and had never had a toy like the one he described having in the other house.

In addition, one night at the dinner table, Chad asked his mother if he would need surgery like the surgery he had before. When she explained to him that he had never had surgery, Chad pointed to the place on his right side where the tissue for James's biopsy had been taken.

Kathy finally showed Chad a picture of James. Her son grinned and his eyes became big, full of amazement. He said that he had been wishing for the picture, and that he wanted it because it was a picture of him. After that,

Kathy sat down with Chad and spoke with him about James. Two days later, Chad came running into the house exclaiming that he could see out of his left eye, something he had not been able to do previously. She had him close his right eye, and he counted her fingers with his left eye. It was a remarkable improvement. Also, she felt her own guilt and grief about James subsiding as she went through the past life experiences with Chad. The entire experience seemed to have a healing effect on both mother and child.

The healing effect that past life regression can have is multifaceted in that it affects more than one person on more than one level. In the case of Kathy, James, and Chad, the boy because of his past life recall was able to use his left eye, and the mother was able to deal with grief she had buried deep within her psyche. Dealing with these issues is how humans move forward physically, mentally, and spiritually.

People were once part of the divine oneness, and through successive lifetimes, hope to again become part of oneness. Energy's natural inclination is to return to its natural and original state, and in this case it is being part of the divine, which is the source of all creation.

If reincarnation has validity, then it means you build each lifetime on what you have created in the previous lifetime and what you create in the next lifetime. Reincarnation is the process that connects your lifetimes together into one. Even though the perspective of past lives and future lives changes, the basic pattern remains the same. The fact that you often seem to keep living lives with certain souls means there is intent in the process of reincarnation. This means that while you are between lifetimes, you essentially choose your parents, and what you expect to accomplish in terms of the whole of who you are.

The healing effect of past life regressions and future life progressions comes from the idea that it connects each lifetime together in terms of the whole of who you are. When negative things happen they can be healed and you can move on in your overall process. You don't need to hold on to the negativity lifetime after lifetime. This is what the healing effects of reincarnation are all about—understanding the individual events of your lifetime in terms of the greater whole, in this case, your eternal spirit.

Who Are You This Lifetime?

Also included in *Return from Heaven* is a case involving two people who basically switched roles within the same lifetime. Margaret was someone everyone thought was wonderful except for her family, whom she mistreated. No one was ever good enough, and she never hesitated to tell them so. Margaret had been beaten as a child, and as a consequence she was always hateful, angry, and domineering to her family. Her youngest daughter, Sarah, was forced to take care of Margaret, and a relationship of love on one hand and conflict on the other resulted. This relationship lasted until Margaret's passing, just before Sarah's wedding, an event that, oddly, had her mother's blessings.

After Sarah had gone through several years of

therapy, worried she would be like Margaret, she finally found herself becoming at peace with her difficult childhood and abusive mother. During this time, Sarah gave birth to two sons, first Kyle and then Miles.

As soon as Miles began to talk, he and Sarah began to fight constantly. This was not in a parent and child fashion; instead Miles berated Sarah for everything she supposedly did wrong. If they tried to do craft projects together, Miles criticized her the whole time until she didn't want to work with him. But interestingly, after each of these times when he was highly judgmental and insulting, he would ask his mother, "If I'm bad, will you still love me? Will you always love me?"

This antagonistic relationship continued until Miles was four years old. He and Sarah were shopping, and Miles saw a print of an elephant that he absolutely had to have. His entire room was filled with elephants. At first Sarah said no, but it did not take long for her to realize she was in a no-win situation, so she bought the picture for him. Upon returning home, Miles immediately hung it on the wall above his bed. Shortly thereafter, the boy showed the picture to his grandfather, Margaret's husband, to which his grandfather responded by saying, "My God! That's a Robert Bateman print! He was your grandmother's favorite artist."

It was at this point that things began to come into focus for Sarah. Her mother loved animals and in particular was obsessed with elephants just as Miles was. Her mother was interested in home decorating, and Miles's favorite shows were the home decorating shows. Also there was

Miles's abusive behavior, which Sarah was beginning to view in a different light. She no longer blamed herself for it.

By the time Miles was six, he and Sarah had created a loving relationship together. The family recently went to an animal park where Miles bonded with a young elephant that normally shies away from people, but was drawn to Miles because of his affinity for elephants.

This case is compelling for several different reasons. It gave Margaret and Sarah as well as Sarah and Miles a second chance to have a harmonious relationship, to get rid of the abusive behavior. Once Sarah realized what was going on, her relationship with Miles went from abusive to harmonious. It also demonstrates that each lifetime offers opportunities to move beyond past problems and negative relationships.

When a child recognizes someone they knew in a past life, continuity exists between how the child reacts in this life and the quality of the relationship in the past life. What it means is that all is not forgotten after death, and that the basic pattern of the relationship tends to remain the same unless something is done to change it.

Many of the studies on reincarnation point to the idea that you, as a person, have certain things you wanted to accomplish when you came into this lifetime. Statistics in regard to the number of past lives within the same family indicate that as a spiritual being you have at least some choice about the body you are born into in each of your lifetimes. Because of this, you have natural inclinations toward certain people, places, and things.

Eastern spiritual traditions and Western studies on reincarnation put forth the idea that you come into this lifetime with certain objectives that you would like to accomplish. This is often why you pick the parents you do. The idea is that by experiencing multiple lifetimes and gaining different knowledge from each, you eventually become whole again; you become divine.

The lessons in life are sometimes pleasurable and sometimes very painful. Most Eastern traditions say that every experience, whether positive or negative, offers the chance to learn. Even deeper is the notion that what makes you who you are is not how you handle the good times, because everyone handles the good times well, but instead how you cope with and handle the bad times. It has been said that you learn more from your failures than you do from your successes. After all, if you don't learn from your failures, then you are doomed to repeat them.

In conjunction with the things you have to learn in each lifetime, you also have things toward which you have natural inclinations. Edgar Cayce once did a reading on a young man. The reading indicated that the man had been involved in designing clothes in another lifetime. When later told about the reading, the man did indeed decide to go into that profession and was very successful. This indicates the possibility that inclinations and patterns in one lifetime carry over into the next lifetime.

As with all energy, there are the inherent polarities of positive and negative. The positive is what you need to work on whether you are a great parent, artist, scientist, or athlete. Everyone has something they are good at. Through time you can usually formulate a pretty good idea of what those things are, such as things you don't have to struggle with in order to be successful at them. Some of these things may be carryovers from other lifetimes.

Along with the positive patterns you need to build upon in each lifetime, you have the negative patterns that you have to work beyond. Patterns, whether positive or negative, that have their root in past lifetimes can progress into future lifetimes unless you choose to end the pattern in your present lifetime. In this sense, it is never too late to make a change because within the continuum of time, everything is relative, depending on your vantage point.

Every day, people do many things that occupy their time. Getting up in the morning, doing things for work, doing things for enjoyment, going to sleep, and so forth, make up a basic progression of life in a day-to-day sense. Beyond this basic progression are the higher levels of what you hope to achieve in the lifetime.

Life with all of its day-to-day rituals is a staging ground for spiritual evolution that we all come back to lifetime after lifetime. The idea is to expand your awareness, and eventually merge with the divine, with oneness.

How to Discover Your Calling

Your calling is your unfolding life purpose. It is what you are here in this lifetime to do. Your calling reflects who you re and how you use your inner potential. It is your life mission that stems from your interests, desires, and personal goals. Formed from your interests, values, and present goals, your calling reflects your many lifetimes, plus your values, actions, beliefs, and sense of who you are.

By identifying and following your life purpose, you can make sure that the goals you pursue are your goals. When you attain them, you are truly glad. Also when you follow your calling, your life journey unfolds with a passion that energizes your body, mind, and spirit.

It is important to make an effort to have a unified commitment to your calling. Once you do this, each day has tremendous direction and purpose. Specific plans start to unfold in your mind on how to attain your life purpose. You wake up excited every morning because you are following your calling in this lifetime.

The following questions are intended to help you discover and follow your calling. Following your calling can give you a profound and personal appreciation of the magic of life. If you already know your calling, this simple exercise will help you clarify your life purpose. I suggest you write down your answers so you can refer to them later.

☾ What are your interests and passions?

☾ What do you love to do so much that you'd pay to do it? You might find clues in the hobbies you enjoy. When you hit upon the things you love to do, you can feel your own inner signals of excitement welling up from the depths of your psyche.

☾ If you had no commitments or responsibilities, what would you be doing, where would you be doing it, and with whom?

☾ What are your core values? What really matters to you?

☾ Think of your loves and desires and the goals you are pursuing now. See your most important goals being achieved. These are the activities of a state of affairs that you are creating. Hold them in your mind's eye, and ask what it is that you value about the goal. Do you value the harmony, happiness, learning, security, love, caring, beauty, sharing, or spiritual grace of the goal?

☾ To you, what is the higher value that all the other values fit into?

Once you identify your calling, answer these questions:

☾ How does your calling relate to your current job?

☾ How does your life purpose relate to your family and friends?

☾ How does your calling relate to you, personally?

☾ What are the implications of your calling?

☾ How does your life purpose relate to your future?

(How does your calling relate to your community?

(Why is following your calling positive for you?

(In what ways does your calling represent who you are, what you care about, and what you think is meaningful in your life?

Now imagine in your mind's eye doing exactly what you like to do. Imagine that you are already following your calling. Steer your awareness in the direction you truly want to take in this lifetime. Imagine these images forming a picture that represents your purpose and calling. Make these images very attractive and exciting. Add lots of details to them. See the images up close, in rich, full, living color.

Then formulate a couple of words or a sentence that describes your calling, your life purpose. Next, step into your calling. Imagine being in various stages of its unfolding. Go ahead and pretend you are really there, as if the future is right now. Enjoy yourself as you see yourself living your life to its fullest potential. Do this for several minutes a day.

Your Eternal Spirit

In *Past Lives, Future Lives*, Dr. Bruce Goldberg describes the case of Henriette Roos, who at an early age in Holland showed great skill as an artist. This was odd since no one in her family had ever displayed artistic talent.

At the age of seventeen, Henriette married Hungarian pianist and composer Franz Weisz. Afterward she submitted some of her art work to the Royal Dutch Academy and was accepted as a student. She graduated with honors, and shortly thereafter divorced her husband, but kept part of his name, calling herself Weisz-Roos because she felt a connection for some reason to the name.

While living in Paris in the summer of 1936, Henriette found she could not sleep, and felt compelled to paint in the dark. For several hours, she labored on a painting that she couldn't see except for the shadows in the darkness. Upon awakening, she found a beautiful portrait of a girl. It was the best painting she had ever done. When she consulted a medium, the woman told the amazed Henriette that it was the great Spanish painter Goya paying her back for past kindness.

Several days afterward, Henriette came across a book on Goya that said a woman named Leucardia Weisz gave Goya asylum when he was exiled from Spain. Her daughter was named Rossaritta Weisz. She was the one who actually looked after Goya. Henriette felt that she had been Rossaritta in a past life. Like Henriette, Rossaritta was a portrait painter. Henriette was carrying on a tradition that was linked through reincarnation. The implications of these kinds of lifetime connections are fascinating and have divine proportions.

If each lifetime is an aspect of your eternal spirit, then there are overall patterns that make you who you are. If the supposition is taken to its logical result, then you have things over lifetimes that you are good at and that you work to be better at. You also have things that you are not so good at in terms of natural skills. These are the skills that you have to improve upon within the karmic whole of who you are as a spiritual whole.

You have an energetic pattern that designates you, much like your physical fingerprint. From lifetime to lifetime, it is what gives you your individual qualities as well as your overall qualities. These are the basic essentials that make you different from every other life form. They make you uniquely you, lifetime after lifetime.

How Reincarnation Can Work for You

The following case from *Past Lives, Future Lives* describes a patient who had suddenly gone blind after witnessing her boyfriend ingesting amphetamines for the first time. The doctors she went to could find no medical reason for her blindness, and she was at a loss as to what to do to regain her sight. Then she turned to hypnotherapy as way to better understand her problem.

She was regressed to a past life in which she lived in the poor section of London around 1887. Her father was a textile worker who drank excessively, so much so that her mother left him because of his drinking. When asked to go back to the possible cause of her current blindness, she went back to an incident when she walked in on her father while he was shooting up morphine. As a consequence, he beat her up and locked her in a closet.

Three minutes after coming out of the past life regression, the patient regained her sight. She realized that catching her boyfriend taking amphetamines had triggered a response in her that was related to this past life. This time, out of self-defense, she decided to go blind and not see, therefore escaping what she saw as the inherent repercussions. By reexperiencing this event in her past life, she was able to perceive what was happening in terms of reincarnation. As a result, she was able to move beyond her blindness. As an added benefit, the claustrophobia that she had experienced from the time she was young also disappeared after the regression.

The healing effects generated through past life regressions and future life progressions happen on many levels. In the instance of the woman who was blind, the child who was blind in one eye, and the man who was schizophrenic, the healing effects could be measured on a very real physical level. In terms of Henriette, the portrait painter, and Sarah and Miles, the healing effects were more psychological, and on some level, most likely karmic. In Henriette's case, she realized her past life connection with the Spanish painter Goya, and in Sarah and Miles's case, they were able to bridge the continuous conflict and abuse in their relationship. The karmic level comes in because both of these cases have a cause and effect relationship that is essentially brought into balance within their current lifetimes.

Use a basic self-hypnosis technique where you decide n a physical or psychological problem you have. Give yourself the suggestion to go back to the root of the problem, whether in this lifetime or a past life. Sometimes the root of a problem can be attributed to more than one incident in this life or past lives. You can use this self-hypnosis technique as way to research your past and future lives, and thus give you greater understanding of why you are who you are.

As a human being, you are a culmination of many things, including genetics, experience, and lifetimes. In terms of genetics and experience, you can look at your ancestors and review the events of your life to get a fairly good perception of how these two factors influence your life. In terms of reincarnation, you often have to dig beneath the surface to find the answers. This is particularly true when genetics and experience can't satisfactorily explain what is happening to you.

Ten Ways to Access Your Lifetimes

One of the most dynamic ways of digging beneath the surface of ordinary reality is applying past life regression and future life progression for personal empowerment. Besides hypnosis and self-hypnosis, there are several other natural avenues for exploring your many lifetimes. The following list provides ten ways you can access your lifetimes.

By applying these methods, you open the door to pe sonal healing, insight, and deeper spiritual understandin Tapping into your lifetimes is a little like tuning into a r wavelength. Meeting your many selves is meeting the sequences of your thoughts, attitudes, and actions, in your many lifetimes as a whole. Be sure to make a note of your experiences for later reference. These notes may prove to be invaluable in your present lifetime.

1. *Creative Meditation*: The easiest method of exploring your many lifetimes is creative meditation, which is why I have included five awareness-expanding meditations in this book. When you meditate on your own without a script, so to speak, simply focus your awareness on moving back in time or moving forward in time. Allow all the sensations and images to flow through you. Make a mental note of those that repeat and those that seem most vivid.

Creative meditation is a sensory, mind-expanding practice. You shape thoughts and images in your mind's eye, and then transmit them to your being as sensory signals and energetic experiences. Form follows thought. All you need is your imagination.

2. *Prayer*: You can use the potent instrument of prayer to call out to the spirit of the universe, to God, Goddess, oneness, by whatever name you choose, to help you tap into your many lifetimes. The word "prayer" means to ask for something. A deeply relaxing form of meditation, prayer is a major communication point between the mortal and divine worlds. It stems from a yearning from within, with empathy and caring as key elements.

Praying creates fields of energy that actually move from the body when you pray. You can use this prayer energy to get in touch with your lifetimes. For example, every morning say this prayer:

> Today and every day, Dear Lord (Lady),
> I pray that I may know my many lifetimes.
> Dear Lord (Lady), I ask you to guide and inspire
>   me.
> Please help me to explore my past and future
>   lifetimes.
> Help me to understand and heal myself with this
>   knowledge
> In this lifetime and in my other lifetimes.
> I ask this in the Lord's (Lady's) name, Amen.

As you say the prayer, feel it as well. Imagine your prayer coming true. See it in your mind's eye, feel it in your senses, and be your prayer with your total self. When done in this way, praying becomes one of the most power-ful ways for you to stimulate past and future lifetime recall. It's a direct line to the divine!

3. *Dreaming*: One of the most natural ways to tap into your many lifetimes is through dreaming. In dreams you often experience the many other yous. Focus on getting more details about your other lifetimes when you dream by giving yourself the suggestion to do exactly that as you drift to sleep. Do this for at least twenty-one nights. Most people have some success within a week. Be sure to phrase your suggestion in the active, as if you are doing the action, dreaming the dream, right now. For example

you want to explore your past lifetimes, as you go to sleep, repeat to yourself,

> *I am dreaming about one of my past lifetimes,*
> *and I remember the details of my dream when I*
> *wake up.*

If you want to dream about your future lifetimes, as you drift to sleep, repeat to yourself,

> *I am dreaming about one of my future lifetimes,*
> *and I remember the details of my dream when I*
> *wake up.*

When you wake up, be sure to write down everything you recall from your dream. Refer to my book *Dream Magic* (HarperSanFrancisco) for more in-depth methods on how to use dreaming to explore your many lifetimes.

4. *Lifetimes Altars*: Create a personal altar or sacred space specifically designed to trigger past and future lifetime recall. Choose a place for your altar that is out of the way and private. I encourage you to change your altar now and again to explore both your past and future lifetimes. Do this by putting pictures, statues, stones, flowers, and candles, as well as jewelry, letters from loved ones and friends, books, or other items you feel strongly attracted to on your lifetime altar. If you want to focus on your ast lives, then create a past life altar using old photos pecially of ancestors), old magazines and newspaper ings, old coins and antique jewelry, as well as other es such as oil lamps, statues, and loving cups. You

can focus further into the past by using runic symbols, tarot cards, pictures of ancient ruins, or images of sacred and magical places around the world.

If you prefer to focus on your future lifetimes, then design your altar accordingly. For example, put a photo of the Earth from space on your altar, sacred geometry images, pictures of fantasy worlds, books about the future, or a clear quartz crystal, as well as magazine pictures of the latest techno-gadgets and other items that symbolize the future to you.

5. *Altered States of Consciousness*: These states of consciousness provide a way to enter the wormholes to other lifetimes. Some of the ways to move into an altered state of consciousness include, but are not limited to, dancing, singing, chanting, listening to music, rhythmic breathing, swimming, running, hiking, and drumming.

6. *Affirmation*: Affirmations are statements of faith and belief that you repeat to yourself with emotional intensity to attain your personal goals. They are useful and easy-to-use tools for accessing your past and future lifetimes. Like prayer, the magic of affirmation comes from the positive intentions and faith you put into the process. The more you reinforce the affirmation on a conscious level, the more your subconscious picks up on it. This initiates change and activates the affirmation. Remember when you recite an affirmation, hold the image of what you want in your mind: see it; feel it; sense it completely; be it! For example, an affirmation for better understanding

your connection with those you love in your present lifetime is

> *Today and every day, I become more aware of the spiritual connections between myself and the people I love, especially my family. Every day I become more and more aware of our divine connection, in this lifetime and in past and future lifetimes. This connection strengthens and empowers me.*

You can also apply this simple three-step affirmation technique to access your many lifetimes.

☾ *Step 1*: Write on the back of your business card, or on a 3 × 5 index card, the words "Every day, in every way, I am more and more aware of my eternal spirit and my many lifetimes. As I recall my past and future lifetimes, they empower and heal me."

☾ *Step 2*: Carry this card with you during the day. Read it out loud five times during the day: at breakfast, lunch, dinner, upon awakening, and just before you go to sleep. Do this for at least twenty-one days in a row, and then as long as you want to continue the experience.

☾ *Step 3*: You will discover the more you do this affirmation, the more you become one with the statement on the card, and the faster you will start exploring your many lifetimes.

7. *Ritual*: During rituals of life such as weddings, birthdays, anniversaries, and funerals, there are occasions when you suddenly get a glimpse into either a future or past lifetime. Many of the people who are closest to you are part of your soul group. When you share experiences with these people in this lifetime, it can stimulate past and future life information.

Also during any kind of ritual, you commune with the divine. This can promote visions of past or future lifetimes. Often this comes in the form of a vivid face in your mind's eye, a name floating around in your head, a geometric pattern, or even a scent from the past or future that momentarily permeates your senses. When this occurs, make a note of it. Often the impressions you receive play themselves out at a later date in your present lifetime. At the very least, they permanently expand your awareness.

8. *Pet Companions, Animals, and Places*: Pet companions such as dogs, cats, birds, and horses can trigger past and future lifetime experiences. For example, a pet Siamese cat companion may trigger past life recall in Egypt. Another example is being drawn to certain breeds of dogs. I am particularly drawn toward beagles. To me, it seems like I've always had little beagle companions in my life, not just in this current lifetime, but in past lifetimes as well.

Like pet companions, certain animals can also trigger past and future lifetime recall. An affinity with wolves, eagles, elephants, tigers, lizards, or other animals may be connected to your many lifetimes. I suggest you keep a picture of any animals you are particularly drawn to on your lifetimes altar. This will stimulate your awareness.

Locales can also precipitate recall of your many lifetimes. I know that I have had a kind of deja vu several times when visiting new places, especially England and Scotland. Just visiting the locale seemed to stimulate my recall of my past lifetimes. In addition, there are instances when you are visiting a place for the first time, yet it seems like you have lived there your whole life. Everything seems so familiar and comfortable, just like home. When this occurs, pay close attention to your responses and thoughts, because it may indicate a past or future life connection.

9. *Gifts*: Once in a while someone gives you a special gift that precipitates some sort of other lifetime recall. It might be a photograph, postcard, old toy, or a piece of jewelry such as a ring or brooch. A gift that can stimulate past or future life recall can be as simple as a single flower given to you by a child. Foods and beverages made from old recipes that have been handed down for hundreds of years can also precipitate recall, sometimes in the form of flashing pictures, a symbol, or a word.

10. *Synchronicity*: This is when two or more things come together at the same time that point to something extraordinary taking place. When synchronistic things occur, it is time to pay close attention to everything around you. Usually you are being given a tremendous clue to your many selves. For example, let's say you turn on the television and it's on a channel with a program about the ancient

ruins of Greece. Then you switch the channel to another station and it just happens to be showing a Hercules cartoon. When you get your mail that day, you receive a catalog with Greek coins for sale. Then while you are driving to the store that same day, you make a wrong turn and find yourself on a street called Athens Court. At this point, you might figure that the universe is trying to tell you something. It's time for you to find out all that you can about ancient Greece and your possible past lifetime(s) there. To do this, use a dream suggestion such as,

> *I am dreaming about my connection with Greece, and any lifetimes I have lived there.*

Other suggestions for stimulating lifetime recall are creating a Greek garden or decorating your home in decor reminiscent of ancient Greece. Spend time in these environments as much as possible. Also, you can eat Greek foods or even take a trip to Greece to get in touch with your possible Greek lifetime(s).

Twenty Benefits to Experiencing Your Lifetimes

The benefits from experiencing past life regression and future life progression have been well documented in the many available books on the subject. These many benefits include but are not limited to the following:

1. *You can live your life in terms of the longer and larger picture, with expanded awareness and personal goals.*

2. You can make better and more insightful decisions for yourself, based on your spiritual connection and the knowledge of your many lifetimes.
3. You can develop a deeper faith in the divine and get in touch with your eternal spirit.
4. You can understand crises, illnesses, and accidents, with regard to other lifetimes, and how they are connected. By doing so, you can keep these challenging times in perspective.
5. You can understand your love relationships with others in a new and more expansive way.
6. You can better understand your children, if you are a parent. You realize that at one time, they were or most likely will be your parents. They are connected to you and are in the same soul group.
7. You can learn to use the information from your past and future lifetimes to heal yourself of physical and psychological problems in your present lifetime.
8. You can learn to better understand your talents and gifts as opportunities to expand yourself. You understand that your unusual aptitudes or your unlearned skills may be linked to other lifetimes.
9. You can deal with questions about birth, life, and death in a more positive and compassionate manner.
10. You can develop a greater respect for yourself and others.

11. You can better understand your circumstances in this lifetime, overcoming obstacles by applying the information from past and future lifetimes.

12. You can better deal with questions regarding your life purpose and the meaning of life.

13. You can become more tolerant of others; your neighbors, coworkers, people from other nations, and so forth.

14. You can gracefully accept your connection to others, to the divine as a part of a greater oneness, by accessing your lifetimes. This connection can empower you.

15. You can see the continuous, eternal aspects of your spirit, your divine nature. You better understand death as a different tense, as a continuing phase of eternal evolution. By doing so, your fear of death diminishes.

16. You can develop a deeper understanding of the things you do each day and why you do what you do.

17. You can better understand your personal goals and dreams.

18. You can cultivate a deeper understanding of nature and the cycles of nature.

19. You can better understand your likes and dislikes, your phobias, behavior patterns, and so forth.

20. You can balance and prioritize your life more effectively, placing emphasis and spending your

time on those things that last the longest, such as love and friendship.

The Three
Faces Meditation

The following creative meditation is designed to put you in touch with your past and future lifetimes. It is most empowering when you tape-record the meditation in your own voice and then play it back. You can do this as many times as you like as a way to explore your many lifetimes. If you prefer, have a close friend read the meditation to you. Or you can read it to yourself, following along a few lines at a time. (See pages 4 and 5 for tips on reading meditations.)

Meditation

BEGIN BY GETTING AS COMFORTABLE AS YOU CAN. SIT BACK OR RECLINE, AND LOOSEN ANY CLOTHING, SHOES, OR JEWELRY THAT MAY BE BINDING YOU. UNCROSS YOUR HANDS AND FEET AND SETTLE INTO THE SURFACE BENEATH YOU.

BREATHE IN TO THE COUNT OF THREE HEART-BEATS, STILL YOUR BREATH FOR THREE HEARTBEATS, AND THEN EXHALE FOR THREE HEARTBEATS. BREATHE THIS WAY FOR A MINUTE OR TWO, BREATHING IN ENERGY, LIGHT, AND RELAXATION, AND BREATHING OUT ANY TENSIONS OR NEGATIVITY YOU MAY BE FEELING.

IF YOU FIND YOURSELF WANTING TO ADJUST

YOUR BODY IN ANY WAY, DO SO NOW, BECOMING MORE AND MORE COMFORTABLE WHILE REMAINING PEACEFULLY AWARE. AS YOU SETTLE IN A LITTLE MORE, CONTINUE TO BREATHE IN AND OUT, SLOWLY AND RHYTHMICALLY.

NOW BEGIN TO SHIFT YOUR ATTENTION TO YOUR FIRST CHAKRA AT THE BASE OF YOUR SPINE. IMAGINE THE COLOR RED IN THIS AREA, IN YOUR ROOT CHAKRA. BREATHE THE COLOR RED INTO THE AREA. THIS IS THE CHAKRA OF SURVIVAL. FEEL YOUR ROOT CHAKRA BECOMING MORE OPEN, STRONGER, AND MORE VITAL AS YOU CONTINUE TO BREATHE THE COLOR OF RED INTO THIS AREA.

NOW TAKE ANOTHER DEEP BREATH AND MOVE YOUR AWARENESS TO YOUR SECOND CHAKRA. THIS IS YOUR EMOTION CHAKRA, WHERE YOU HAVE THE ABILITY TO FEEL WHAT OTHERS FEEL. OPEN THIS CHAKRA TO THE EMPOWERING ENERGIES OF THE UNIVERSE. NOW IMAGINE THE COLOR ORANGE IN THIS AREA. BREATHE THE COLOR ORANGE INTO YOUR SECOND CHAKRA. FEEL THE BALANCE, HARMONY, AND THE CALM RELAXATION OF EACH DEEP BREATH AS YOU BREATHE THE COLOR ORANGE IN AND OUT OF THIS CHAKRA.

VERY SLOWLY MOVE YOUR AWARENESS TO YOUR SOLAR PLEXUS, YOUR THIRD CHAKRA CALLED YOUR POWER CHAKRA. THIS IS WHERE YOU GENERATE ACTION. BREATHE THE COLOR GOLD INTO THIS AREA. IN YOUR MIND'S EYE, IMAGINE THE BRIGHT SUN SHIN-

ING IN YOUR SOLAR PLEXUS. BREATHE IN THE SOLAR ENERGY, THE POWER OF THE SUN, TO ENERGIZE THIS AREA.

SLOWLY FOCUS YOUR AWARENESS ON YOUR HEART CHAKRA, BREATHING IN THE COLOR GREEN. IMAGINE THE GREEN OF NATURE, OF TREES, AND BRIGHT GREEN GRASS IN YOUR HEART AREA. NOW TAKE A DEEP BREATH AND IMAGINE A BEAUTIFUL ROSE-COLORED ROSE IN YOUR HEART CHAKRA. SENSE A FEELING OF OPENNESS, OF BALANCE OF HARMONY, IN THIS AREA AS YOU CONTINUE TO IMAGINE A BEAUTIFUL ROSE-COLORED ROSE IN YOUR HEART CHAKRA.

NOW SLOWLY MOVE YOUR AWARENESS TO YOUR THROAT CHAKRA, IMAGINING THE COLOR BLUE, THE COLOR OF WATER AND THE SKY. THIS IS THE AREA OF COMMUNICATION, TELEPATHY, AND CLAIRAUDI-ENCE. YOUR SENSES OF TASTE AND SMELL RESIDE HERE. BREATHE THE COLOR BLUE INTO YOUR THROAT CHAKRA, FEELING YOUR THROAT OPENING AND RELAXING WITH EACH BREATH YOU TAKE.

NOW SLOWLY SHIFT YOUR ATTENTION TO YOUR THIRD EYE, IMAGINING THE COLOR VIOLET FILLING YOUR FOREHEAD BETWEEN YOUR BROWS. THIS IS WHERE KNOWINGNESS AND CLAIRVOYANCE RESIDE. FOCUS ON BREATHING THE COLOR VIOLET INTO YOUR THIRD EYE. OPEN YOURSELF TO THE ENERGY AND HARMONY OF THE UNIVERSE.

MOVE YOUR AWARENESS UPWARD TO YOUR

CROWN CHAKRA, TO THE TOP OF YOUR HEAD, WHERE YOU ARE CONNECTED WITH THE UNIVERSAL WISDOM AND ONENESS. NOW BREATHE PURE WHITE LIGHT INTO YOUR CROWN CHAKRA. BREATHE IN WHITE, THE COLOR THAT CONTAINS ALL OTHER COLORS, THE COLOR OF ONENESS. FOCUS ON BREATHING IN AND FILLING THE TOP OF YOUR HEAD WITH RADIANT WHITE ENERGY.

AS YOU BREATHE THESE COLORS INTO YOUR BODY, INTO YOUR BEING, YOU BALANCE YOUR MIND, BODY, AND SPIRIT. ALLOW YOURSELF TO EXPERIENCE THE HARMONY OF THE UNIVERSE AS YOU CONTINUE TO BREATHE IN AND BREATHE OUT, RELAXING MORE AND MORE WITH EACH BREATH YOU TAKE.

AS YOU TAKE ANOTHER DEEP BREATH, BEGIN TO IMAGINE A SINGLE POINT OF WHITE LIGHT IN YOUR MIND'S EYE. NOTICE THE LIGHT BECOMING BRIGHTER AND CLEARER AS YOU MOVE TOWARD IT. THE WHITE LIGHT FEELS WARM AND INVITING, COMFORTABLE AND SOOTHING. AS YOU MOVE CLOSER TO THE LIGHT, YOU FEEL DRAWN TO ITS WARMTH.

IMAGINE WALKING INTO THE INVITING LIGHT. IN A FLASH, YOU FIND YOURSELF STANDING AT THE BOTTOM OF A CRYSTAL STAIRWAY. YOU TAKE A DEEP BREATH, AND THEN BEGIN SLOWLY WALKING UP THE CRYSTAL STAIRS, ONE AT A TIME. THE LIGHT SHINES ODDLY THROUGH THE BOTTOM OF THE STEPS AS YOU MOVE EVER UPWARD. THE CRYSTAL STAIRS AND RAIL ARE SEAMLESS AS IF HEWN FROM ONE IMMENSE

STONE, AND THE STONE RAIL FEELS SMOOTH AND
SEEMS TO SWEAT UNDER YOUR HAND AS YOU MOVE
UP THE STAIRWAY.

AT THE TOP OF THE STAIRWAY, YOU PAUSE,
LOOKING IN FRONT OF YOU AT A GARDEN OF MAGIC
AND WONDER. THE FLOWERS, TREES, AND PLANTS
SEEM FAMILIAR, YET STRANGE, AND THE SOUNDS OF
THE BIRD SONG ECHO MYSTERIOUSLY IN THE BEAUTI-
FUL GARDEN.

YOU WALK UNDER A MAGNIFICENT CRYSTAL
ARCHWAY COVERED WITH THICK VINES OF WILDLY
COLORED AND FRAGRANT FLOWERS. AS YOU
ENTER THE GARDEN, A SOFT BREEZE GREETS AND
REFRESHES YOU AS IT SOFTLY CARESSES YOUR FACE
AND BODY.

THE GARDEN IS FILLED WITH A CLEAR AND
BRIGHT LIGHT, AND EVERYTHING SHIMMERS AND
SHINES BEFORE YOU. BREATHING DEEPLY, YOU RELAX
A LITTLE MORE AS YOU MOVE YOUR AWARENESS
AROUND THE GARDEN. TREES OF EVERY VARIETY FILL
THE MAGIC GARDEN, BLENDED WITH THICK, LUSH
PLANTS AND BUSHES. MORE WILDLY COLORED
FLOWERS SPILL ON THE GROUND HERE AND THERE
LIKE NATURAL JEWELS, AND THEIR SWEET AROMA
STIRS YOUR SENSES. AS YOU CONTINUE TO SLOWLY
WALK THROUGH THE GARDEN, THE STRONG SCENT OF
WILD HERBS FILLS THE AIR. YOU CHERISH THE SENSA-
TION AS YOU BREATHE IN THE HEADY SCENT.

HEARING THE SOUND OF RUNNING WATER NEAR-

BY, YOU HEAD TOWARD THE SOUND AND DISCOVER A SMALL POOL OF WATER FED BY A NATURAL SPRING. SITTING DOWN COMFORTABLY ON THE MOSSY EDGE OF THE POOL, YOU DIP YOUR HAND IN THE CLEAR WATER. IT FEELS COOL AND SLIPPERY TO THE TOUCH.

YOU PICK UP A FEW SMALL STONES ON THE GROUND NEXT TO YOU, AND THEY FEEL UNUSUALLY WARM TO THE TOUCH. YOU HOLD THEM MOMENTARILY BEFORE TOSSING THEM INTO THE SMALL POOL. WITH EACH STONE YOU TOSS, YOU WATCH THE RIPPLES MOVE SLOWLY AND RHYTHMICALLY OUT FROM THE CENTER OF THE POOL TO ITS BANK.

AS YOU WATCH THE RIPPLES, YOU FIND YOURSELF BECOMING MORE AND MORE RELAXED, OPENING UP YOUR SENSES, YET REMAINING PEACEFULLY ALERT AND CALM. THE STRANGE ECHOING SOUNDS OF THE MOVING WATER AND THE BIRD SONG SOOTHE YOU EVEN MORE.

THE CLEAR, STILL WATER OF THE POOL ACTS AS A NATURAL MIRROR. YOU CAN SEE THE SURROUNDING TREES AND PLANTS ALL PERFECTLY REFLECTED IN ITS GLASSY SURFACE. WITH EACH BREATH YOU TAKE, LIKE THE OTHER REFLECTIONS IN THE POOL, YOUR IMAGE AND FACE BECOME CLEARER AND BETTER DEFINED IN ITS GLASSY SURFACE. LOOKING INTO YOUR OWN MIRRORED FACE, YOU NOTICE AS MANY DETAILS ABOUT YOUR IMAGE AS YOU CAN.

AS YOU CONTINUE TO LOOK INTO THE MIRRORED SURFACE OF THE POOL, ALLOW THE WISE SPIRIT

WITHIN YOURSELF TO REGRESS BACK IN TIME AND
SELECT A PAST LIFETIME TO EXPERIENCE, ONE THAT
HAS SOMETHING OF VALUE TO SHOW YOU. IN YOUR
MIND'S EYE SLOWLY BEGIN TO IMAGINE ANOTHER
FACE, A FACE BEHIND YOUR FACE IN THE MIRRORED
POOL. THIS FACE IS ANOTHER YOU, A YOU IN A PAST
LIFETIME.

TAKE A FEW MOMENTS TO NOTICE AS MANY OF
THE DETAILS AND NUANCES OF THIS OTHER YOU AS
YOU CAN. NOW MERGE WITH AND SHAPE SHIFT INTO
THIS OTHER FACE, THIS PAST YOU, FOR A FEW
MOMENTS. TRY ON THIS OTHER, PAST LIFETIME FACE
IN YOUR MIND'S EYE.

NOW TAKE A DEEP BREATH AND FOCUS ALL OF
YOUR AWARENESS ON THIS PAST LIFETIME. BECOME
THIS OTHER YOU IN THIS PAST LIFETIME. NOW BRIEFLY
LOOK DOWN AT YOUR HANDS. ARE YOU WEARING
ANY RINGS OR OTHER JEWELRY? LOOK DOWN AT
YOUR FEET. WHAT KIND OF SHOES, IF ANY, ARE YOU
WEARING? NOW SCAN YOUR BODY AND CLOTHES
(IF YOU ARE WEARING ANY). ARE YOU A WOMAN OR
MAN? WHAT COLOR IS YOUR SKIN? LOOK AROUND
YOU. WHAT DOES THE LANDSCAPE LOOK LIKE?
ARE THERE BUILDINGS, OTHER BEINGS, PLANTS, OR
ANIMALS? WHAT COLOR IS THE SKY? HOW MANY
SUNS OR MOONS ARE IN THE SKY? WHAT YEAR DOES
IT SEEM TO BE? IF YOU CAN, MAKE AN EFFORT TO
FIND OUT WHAT YOUR NAME IS AS THIS PAST YOU.
WHAT IS IT THAT YOU DO IN THIS PAST LIFETIME?

Who are the people you love in this past lifetime, and who loves you? What is most important to you in this past lifetime?

Focus all your attention on being this other you and make a mental note of what it feels like. Now ask this you to show you something that can be used to help you in your present lifetime. Pay close attention to the suggestion or illumination. Make a mental note of the communication.

Now take a deep and complete breath and shift your awareness back to the magic garden and the mirrored pool. Once again, look into its surface. Allow your wise spirit within to progress forward in time and select a future lifetime to explore, one that has something of value to show you.

Very slowly begin imagining a third face, a future you, being reflected in the mirrored surface of the pool of water. Merge with and shape shift into this future you, with this image of yourself in a future lifetime. Become one with this third face, this future you.

Now take a deep breath and focus all your awareness on this future you. Now, slowly look down at your hands. Notice any rings or other jewelry on your hands. Look down at your feet. What kind of shoes, if any, do you have on? Scan your body. Are you a woman or

MAN? WHAT KIND OF CLOTHES, IF ANY, ARE YOU WEARING? WHAT COLOR IS YOUR SKIN? LOOK AROUND YOU. DO YOU KNOW WHERE YOU ARE? DOES ANYTHING LOOK FAMILIAR? WHAT DOES THE LANDSCAPE LOOK LIKE? ARE THERE BUILDINGS, OTHER BEINGS, PLANTS, AND ANIMALS, OR ARE YOU ON SOME STRANGE NEW WORLD? WHAT COLOR IS THE SKY? HOW MANY SUNS OR MOONS ARE IN THE SKY? WHAT IS IT YOU DO IN THIS FUTURE LIFETIME? HOW DO YOU SPEND YOUR DAYS AND NIGHTS? WHO ARE THE PEOPLE YOU LOVE IN THIS FUTURE LIFETIME, AND WHO LOVES YOU? WHAT IS MOST IMPORTANT TO YOU IN THIS FUTURE LIFETIME?

ONCE AGAIN, ASK THIS FUTURE YOU TO SHOW YOU SOMETHING THAT CAN BE USED TO HELP YOU IN YOUR PRESENT LIFETIME. MAKE A MENTAL NOTE OF WHAT YOU ARE SHOWN.

NOW SLOWLY BEGIN INTEGRATING THESE THREE FACES OF FUTURE, PAST, AND PRESENT LIFETIMES IN THE MIRRORED POOL INTO ONE. MERGE THEM TOGETHER INTO YOUR BEING BY IMAGINING THE FACES MERGING INTO ONE BRILLIANT REFLECTION IN THE POOL'S GLASSY SURFACE. WITH THIS HARMONY OF YOUR FACES, YOUR SELVES, AND LIFETIMES, ALLOW YOURSELF TO FEEL AT ONE WITH THE MANY YOUS. SPEND A FEW MOMENTS INTEGRATING YOUR FACES INTO ONE. NOW IMAGINE THE BRILLIANT REFLECTION IN THE POOL BECOMING YOU—THE YOU RIGHT NOW, THE YOU OF YOUR PRESENT LIFETIME.

WHEN YOU ARE FINISHED LOOKING INTO THE
MIRRORED POOL, INTO YOUR OWN MIRRORED FACE
AND YOUR OTHER LIFETIMES OF AWARENESS, TAKE A
DEEP BREATH. IN YOUR MIND'S EYE, IMAGINE GETTING
UP FROM THE MOSSY EDGE OF THE POOL AND START-
ING TO MOVE THROUGH THE LUSH MAGIC GARDEN.
YOU WALK SLOWLY THROUGH THE MAGNIFICENT
CRYSTAL ARCHWAY, AND OVER TO THE TOP OF THE
CRYSTAL STAIRWAY.

BREATHE DEEPLY AND BEGIN TO DESCEND THE
STAIRWAY, ONE STEP AT A TIME, KNOWING YOU CAN
RETURN TO THIS MAGIC GARDEN WHENEVER YOU
WANT TO LEARN MORE ABOUT YOUR MANY FACES
AND LIFETIMES. TAKE ANOTHER DEEP BREATH AND
MAKE AN EFFORT TO REMEMBER WHAT WAS SHOWN
TO YOU FROM PAST AND FUTURE LIFETIMES.

IN YOUR MIND'S EYE, STEP BACK INTO THE WHITE
LIGHT, BATHING IN ITS SOOTHING WARMTH FOR A FEW
MOMENTS. ALLOW ITS HEALING RADIANCE TO COM-
PLETELY FILL YOU UP. IMAGINE THE LIGHT ACTIVATING
ALL OF YOUR NATURAL HEALING AND CREATIVE ABIL-
ITIES. ALLOW THE LIGHT TO INSPIRE AND GUIDE YOU
TODAY, TOMORROW, IN THIS LIFETIME, AND IN ALL
LIFETIMES. TAKE A FEW MOMENTS NOW TO REFLECT
ON YOUR MANY FACES AND LIFETIMES AS WELL AS
THE BEAUTY AND WISDOM THAT COME FROM THEM.

FEELING FULL OF ENERGY, YET RELAXED AND
CALM, NOW SLOWLY TAKE ANOTHER DEEP BREATH
AND BEGIN FOCUSING YOUR ATTENTION ON YOUR

BODY. MOVE YOUR TOES AND FEET, YOUR HANDS AND FINGERS, AND SLOWLY OPEN YOUR EYES. COME BACK TO THE ROOM COMPLETELY, STRETCHING YOUR BODY AND FOCUSING ON YOUR IMMEDIATE ENVIRONMENT.

☞ *Be sure to write down the different faces and lifetimes you experienced. Include every detail you can recall. Most likely, you will be able to apply the information you gleaned from the meditation in a way that will benefit your present lifetime.*

Bibliography

Bancroft, Anne. *Religions of the East*. New York: St. Martin's Press, 1974.

Banerjee, H. N., and Will Oursler. *Lives Unlimited: Reincarnation East and West*. New York: Doubleday, 1974.

Benson, Herbert, and Miriam Klipper. *The Relaxation Response*. New York: Avon, 1976.

Berstein, Morey. *The Search for Bridey Murphy*. New York: Doubleday, 1956.

Bowman, Carol. *Children's Past Lives*. New York: Bantam Books, 1997.

Bowman, Carol. *Return from Heaven: Beloved Relative Reincarnated Within Your Family*. New York: HarperCollins, 2001.

Brown, Daniel, and Erika Fromm. *Hynotherapy and Hypnoanalysis*. Hillsdale, NJ: Lawrence Erilbaum, 1986.

Buhlman, William. *The Secret of the Soul*. New York: Harper-SanFrancisco, 2001.

Cayce, Edgar. *You Can Remember Your Past Lives*. New York: Warner Books, 1989.

Chopra, Deepak. *The Seven Spiritual Laws for Parents*. New York: Harmony Books, 1997.

Cockell, Jenny. *Across Time and Death*. New York: Simon & Schuster, 1993.

Cranston, Sylvia, and Carey Williams. *Reincarnation: A New Horizon in Science, Religion, and Society*. New York: Julian Press, 1984.

Eadie, Betty J. *Embraced by the Light*. Placerville, CA: Gold Leaf Press, 1992.

Evans-Wentz, W. Y., trans. *The Tibetan Book of the Dead*. London: Oxford University Press, 1960.

Eyre, Richard. *Life Before Life*. Salt Lake City, UT: Shadow Mountain, 2000.

Fiore, Edith. *The Unquiet Dead*. New York: Ballantine Books, 1988.

Fiore, Edith. *You Have Been Here Before*. New York: Ballantine Books, 1978.

Gershom, Yonassan. *Beyond the Ashes*. Virgina Beach, VA: ARE Press, 1992.

Godwin, Malcolm. *The Lucid Dreamer*. New York: Simon & Schuster, 1994.

Goldberg, Bruce. *Past Lives, Future Lives*. New York: Ballantine Books, 1988.

Guirdham, Arthur. *The Cathars and Reincarnation*. Woodstock, NY: Beekman Publishing, Inc., 1992.

Hamilton-Parker, Craig. *What to Do When You Are Dead*. New York: Sterling Publishing Co., Inc., 2001.

Hammerman, David, and Lisa Lenard. *The Complete Idiot's Guide to Reincarnation*. Indianapolis, IN: Alpha Books, 2000.

Harrison, Peter and Mary. *The Children That Time Forgot*. New York: Berkeley Publishing Group, 1991.

Head, Joseph, and Sylvia Cranston. *Reincarnation: The Phoenix Fire Mystery*. Pasedena, CA: Theosophical University Press, 1994.

Holtzer, Hans. *Life Beyond Life*. New York: Parker Publishing, 1985.

Ingerman, Sandra. *Soul Retrieval*. San Francisco, CA: HarperSan-Francisco, 1991.

Johnson, Christopher Jay, Ph.D., and Marsha G. McGee. *How Different Religions View Death and Afterlife*. Philadelphia, PA: The Charles Press, 1998.

Jung, Carl G. *The Archetypes of the Collective Unconscious*. Princeton, NJ: Princeton University Press, 1990.

Jung, Carl G. *Synchronicity*. Princeton, NJ: Princeton University Press, 1973.

Kabat-Zinn, Jon. *Wherever You Go, There You Are*. New York: Hyperion, 1994.

Knight, Sirona. *Celtic Traditions*. New York: Citadel Press, 2000.

Knight, Sirona. *Dream Magic: Night Spells and Rituals for Love, Prosperity, and Personal Power*. San Francisco, CA: HarperSanFrancisco, 2000.

Knight, Sirona. *The Pocket Guide to Celtic Spirituality*. Freedom, CA: Crossing Press, 1998.

Knight, Sirona. *The Pocket Guide to Crystals and Gemstones*. Freedom, CA: Crossing Press, 1998.

Lawson, Lee. *Visitations from the Afterlife*. New York: HarperSanFrancisco, 2000.

Leach, Maria, ed. *Standard Dictionary of Folklore, Mythology, and Legend.* New York: Funk & Wagnalls Co., 1950.

Linn, Denise. *The Secret Language of Signs.* New York: Ballantine Books, 1996.

Maguire, Jack. *Essential Buddhism.* New York: Pocket Books, 2001.

McDermott, Robert, ed. *The Essential Aurobindo.* Great Barrington, MA: Lindisfarne Press, 2001.

Meek, George W. *After We Die, What Then?* London: Metascience Corporation, 1990.

Montgomery, Ruth. *Threshold to Tomorrow.* New York: Fawcett Crest, 1982.

Montgomery, Ruth. *The World Before.* New York: Fawcett Crest, 1976.

Moody, Raymond. *Life After Life.* New York: Bantam Books, 1975.

Neiman, Carol, and Emily Goldman. *Afterlife.* New York: Viking Studio Books, 1994.

Newton, Michael. *Journey of Souls.* St. Paul, MN: Llewellyn Publications, 1994.

Van Praagh, James. *Reaching to Heaven.* New York: Dutton, 1999.

Prabhavananda, Swami, and Frederick Manchester, eds. *The Upanishads.* New York: New American Library, 1957.

Ring, Kenneth. *The Omega Project.* New York: William Morrow, 1992.

Rinpoche, Sogyal. *The Tibetan Book of Living and Dying.* New York: HarperCollins, 1994.

Sheldrake, Rupert. *The Presence of the Past.* Rochester, VT: Park Street Press, 1988.

Sheldrake, Rupert. *The Rebirth of Nature.* Rochester, VT: Park Street Press, 1991.

Shroder, Tom. *A Matter of Death and Life.* New York: Simon & Schuster, 1990.

Shroder, Tom. *Old Souls: The Scientific Evidence for Past Lives.* New York: Simon & Schuster, 1999.

Siblerud, Robert. *The Science of the Soul.* Willington, CO: Sacred Science Publications, 2000.

Simpkins, C. Alexander and Annellen. *Simple Buddhism*. Boston, MA: Tuttle Publishing, 2000.

Simpkins, C. Alexander and Annellen. *Simple Confucianism*. Boston, MA: Tuttle Publishing, 2000.

Smith, Huston. *The World's Religions*. New York: Harper SanFrancisco, 1991.

Stevenson, Ian. *Cases of the Reincarnation Type, Vol. I: India*. Charlottesville, VA: University Press of Virginia, 1975.

Stevenson, Ian. *Children Who Remember Previous Lives*. Charlottesville, VA: University Press of Virginia, 1987.

Stevenson, Ian. *Twenty Cases Suggestive of Reincarnation*. Charlottesville, VA: University Press of Virginia, 1974.

Talbot, Michael. *Your Past Lives*. New York: Fawcett Crest, 1987.

Taub, Edward. *Seven Steps to Self-Healing*. New York: DK Publishing, Inc., 1996.

Tribble, Frank, ed. *An Arthur Ford Anthology*. Nevada City, CA: Blue Dophin Publishing, 1999.

Wambach, Helen. *Life Before Life*. New York: Bantam Books, 1979.

Wambach, Helen. *Reliving Past Lives*. New York: Bantam Books, 1979.

Weiss, Brian. *Through Time Into Healing*. New York: Simon & Schuster, 1992.

Wells, H. G. *The Outline of History*. Garden City, NY: Garden City Books, 1961.

Woolger, Roger. *Other Lives, Other Selves*. New York: Bantam Books, 1988.

Zukav, Gary. *The Seat of the Soul*. New York: Fireside, 1989.